Become an English Teacher

Essential tools, strategies and methodologies
for building a successful business

Nestor Kiourtzidis

Packed with practical advice, marketing tips, and lesson ideas

Pavilion e?t

Become an Online English Teacher: Essential tools, strategies and methodologies for building a successful business

© Nestor Kiourtzidis

The author has asserted his rights in accordance with the Copyright, Designs and Patents Act (1988) to be identified as the author of this work.

Published by:
Pavilion Publishing and Media Ltd
Blue Sky Offices Shoreham,
25 Cecil Pashley Way,
Shoreham-by-Sea,
BN43 5FF

Tel:	+44 (0)1273 434 943
Email:	info@pavpub.com
Website:	www.pavpub.com

First published 2015. Reprinted 2016, 2018 and 2020.

A catalogue record for this book is available from the British Library.

ISBN: 978-1-910366-77-6

Author: Nestor Kiourtzidis
ELT development editor: Penny Hands
Production editor: Catherine Ansell-Jones, Pavilion Publishing and Media Ltd
Cover design: Emma Dawe, Pavilion Publishing and Media Ltd
Layout design: Emma Dawe, Pavilion Publishing and Media Ltd
Printing: Severn Print

Contents

Acknowledgements

I wish to personally thank the following people for their contributions to my inspiration and knowledge in creating this book:

Austin Wood

Polina Kuzina

Nicola Freeborough

Penny Hands

Introduction

The practice of teaching and learning English online is growing rapidly in importance and popularity. This sudden expansion is due to a number of factors:

- the continual development of high bandwidth broadband internet
- the widespread availability of free Voice over Internet Protocol (VoIP) communication tools such as Skype
- the social shift towards virtual communication
- a shortage of English teachers in high-demand countries.

This book is for readers intending to establish their own online one-to-one tutoring service, as well as those currently teaching online. It is the result of the author's own experience as well as interviews and correspondence with successful teachers. A range of practical information is covered, including:

- essential online tools and applications (Chapter 1)
- effective tactics for finding students online (Chapter 2)
- actionable steps on how to set up a blog for your service (Chapter 3)
- best practices for promoting your blog (Chapter 4)
- recommended procedures for enrolling new students (Chapter 5)
- efficient methods for processing online payments (Chapter 6)
- practical lesson ideas and resources (Chapter 7).

For freelance English tutors, teaching online offers a number of attractive incentives as well as potential drawbacks. First, let's consider the benefits.

Why teach online?

Convenience

A key benefit of teaching online is that both teacher and student are not physically limited to their local area for the lessons to take place. Tuition can be conducted in practically any quiet environment where there is a reliable internet connection. In addition to workplace mobility, teaching online allows you to schedule lessons any time of the day or night depending on the time zones in which your prospective students are located. This means that you can arrange lessons outside of traditional tuition hours, eg. late at night or early in the morning. This is handy if you want to fit your online lessons around a day job or study schedule. Online teaching also eliminates the need to arrange or tidy the workspace in preparation for your next student, which means that you can instantly stop what you are doing and begin teaching.

Your personality type

Another potential reason for teaching online may be your personality type. Teaching a traditional classroom of students is generally considered to favour a more extroverted type of teacher. Although introverts do have the ability to act out of character when teaching, according to Harvard professor Brian Little in his entertaining TEDxTalk in May 2014, the playing field is significantly levelled when it comes to one-to-one lessons. Online one-to-one tuition, which involves greater physical distance between the teacher and student, can even appeal to shy introverts – people who normally tend to struggle to approach others and make conversation with them. In short, practically any personality type can thrive as an online teacher.

Skills development

As you grow as an online teacher, hopefully by implementing the ideas and strategies outlined in this book, you will develop invaluable internet skills that can be applied to other fields of work. These include building a professional-looking website without requiring a deep knowledge of coding, blogging and promoting yourself with the latest internet marketing techniques and becoming more web-savvy in general. With the development and widespread use of mobile devices and laptops, the internet is likely to continue to grow in importance as a marketing channel for any business. Therefore, a broad practical understanding of this medium may serve you well in the future should you ever grow out of teaching.

Financial reasons

The potential to earn more money as an online teacher might be another motivating factor. If you live in a country where the standard hourly rate for face-to-face tuition is relatively low, you might be able to earn a higher income as an online teacher by targeting students from wealthier countries. Even if you do earn a decent income from traditional lessons, the ability to take on students outside normal tuition hours will allow you to increase your monthly revenue.

Potential drawbacks

Financial

As we have seen, online teaching can be attractive to teachers working in countries where face-to-face rates are low. However, it can be less attractive to aspiring online teachers who live in a country where the cost of private tuition is relatively high. In such cases, a teacher may struggle to charge the same fees online (at least in the short term). One solution is to focus on a particular niche market and develop a reputation; in this way, a teacher can justify charging much higher fees online. Pricing and strategies designed to enhance a teacher's credibility are discussed in Chapters 2, 3 and 4.

Marketing effort

Compared to local freelance tuition, running a successful online teaching business requires a significantly greater marketing effort. Local tutors often promote themselves by posting a simple classified ad, and they usually have to compete with only a few other teachers. Online teachers, on the other hand, typically have to contend with more intense competition (even though their advertisement is likely to be viewed by a far greater number of prospective students). They will therefore need to develop their internet marketing skills and spend more time promoting themselves (at least in the first 6–12 months). As stated earlier, this challenge can also been seen as an incentive to the teacher who wants to widen his or her professional horizons. Chapters 2–4 cover the marketing aspects of running an online teaching business.

Interaction

There are key differences between face-to-face and online interaction. In a traditional setting, the teacher and student can see each other and physically interact with the workspace and lesson resources. In an online setting, the teacher and student may not see each other, and even if video calling is enabled, the field of view is limited and physical interaction is still impossible. Thus, a number of activities that face-to-face teachers take for granted are either hindered or rendered impossible during remote online tuition. These include:

- monitoring and observing the student during silent activities (reading, writing, listening)
- illustrating key concepts with pen and paper or on a whiteboard
- using body language to reinforce meaning
- reading the student's body language to check understanding
- simplifying instructions with gestures (eg. pointing to an exercise)
- playing board games, using paper-based flashcards and conducting other physical lesson activities.

These physical and visual drawbacks mean that online teachers will need to rely more heavily on speech and will need to develop their verbal communication skills and ability to read auditory signals such as the student's tone of voice. The online teacher will often need to verbally check understanding, and so a basic knowledge of the student's mother tongue will be of great benefit with low-level learners. The other obstacles mentioned above can be mitigated to a certain extent using tools and techniques that will be explored in this book.

Technological barriers

Although the technology is continually developing, high-speed broadband internet is still not universally available. Even if your own connection speed meets the minimum requirements for a high-quality voice or video call (see Chapter 1), your student's connection might not be as fast or reliable. According to 2012 data compiled by the International Telecommunication Union, the percentage of each country's population subscribing to wired and mobile cellular internet can vary considerably. In Saudi Arabia, for example, 6.8% of the population are wired internet subscribers whereas 42.8% have a mobile cellular subscription. This means that the quality of calls with many Saudi Arabian users will depend on their mobile internet connection speeds. In addition to potential call quality issues, the total number of lessons that you are able to teach online every month may be restricted if you are on a limited data plan (see page 11).

Despite these challenges, online teaching can be successful and rewarding for both teacher and student. The tips, ideas and strategies presented here should benefit not only aspiring online tutors but also those who already have some experience. Readers who are new to teaching online can use this book as a one-stop guide to setting up, promoting and delivering a successful online tutoring service, while experienced teachers wanting to increase their revenue may benefit significantly from the marketing information provided.

Chapter 1:

Tools of the trade

Tools play a vital role in online teaching success. This chapter presents the devices and applications that will enable you to run a smooth service and make the most efficient use of your time. These include several indispensable free tools that will help you convey competence to your students and make your life easier as an online tutor.

Hardware

It is not necessary to have the very latest hardware to provide an effective online English course; most available devices and operating systems are adequate. Using a smartphone, however, is generally not recommended, unless you are providing a simple conversation course and using an external headset. Mobile versions of applications usually come with limited features, and the small screen size makes the learning process considerably more awkward.

In order to teach online effectively, the following hardware is recommended:

- a computer or tablet, preferably a laptop or desktop computer
- a webcam (if your device is not equipped with a built-in video camera)
- a quality headset equipped with an external microphone.

Using a headset rather than your device's built-in speakers and microphone will ensure better audio quality and reduce background noise and echo. Consider investing in a wireless headset for greater physical mobility. Teaching online can be very sedentary work, especially if you are taking on a full schedule, and you will welcome the freedom to move around or stretch from time to time.

COMMUNICATION TOOLS

Skype™ (www.skype.com)

Skype is currently the most widely used Voice over Internet Protocol (VoIP) application with over 600 million users worldwide. It is the platform of choice for most online tutors. Although there is a plethora of other free VoIP software products, Skype is distinguished by three important factors:

- Popularity: if students are already familiar with a particular application, there are fewer perceived obstacles to learning online.

- Quality: the highest possible voice and video quality will help avoid a frustrating experience for both learner and teacher.

- Desktop compatibility: not all VoIP applications are suitable for non-mobile devices, and larger screens are still more convenient for sending files, making video calls and doing collaborative exercises.

For the online teacher, Skype offers a number of useful features including free video calls, voice calls, instant messaging and screen sharing. You can create your own username and also edit the names of your contacts. In addition, plugin support allows you to add numerous extensions for added functionality. For example, the PrettyMay extension makes it possible to record calls (which is useful for recording activities) and to share audio during a conversation (which is handy for playing dialogues).

Setting up your Skype business account

Assuming that you are already a Skype user, it is a good idea to set up a separate Skype account for your online business. Apart from allowing you to separate your personal contacts from your business, a secondary Skype account will help you establish your brand and promote your service.

Go to https://login.skype.com/account/signup-form and sign up for a new account. Choose an appropriate Skype name for your business, preferably one that is easy to remember with the word 'English' in it. This will serve as your brand name. If you are going to create a website to publicise your service (see Chapter 3), you might want to create a username that matches your domain name.

If you are using a desktop or laptop, you don't need to sign out of your private Skype account in order to use your new business account. Both accounts can be run on the same computer at the same time by following the steps outlined in the Appendix.

Renaming contacts

Skype allows you to edit the names of your contacts by right-clicking on a contact and selecting **Rename**. This is a convenient function because once your contact list grows, you may need to adopt a renaming convention in order to keep track of your students and potential clients. For example, you could append 'PS' to a username to indicate a potential student.

Sharing files

Skype makes it possible to instantly send a file to a contact. The feature enables online tutors to conveniently share downloadable resources such as pdf worksheets and audio files. Unfortunately, not all devices fully support Skype file transfers. At the time of writing, iPhone and iPad users can only accept image files. However, there are alternative instant file-sharing tools, such as Dropbox (see page 13).

Sharing your screen

Using Skype's screen-sharing function, you can display resources such as pdf worksheets, images and silent video. The advantage of showing the student a resource rather than giving instructions ('Go to the next page', 'Scroll down to Exercise 3', etc.) is that you are in control of the student's field of view, which avoids unnecessary confusion and delays. This feature comes in handy when teaching lower level learners, who are more likely to misunderstand your instructions.

Keyboard shortcuts

During a Skype lesson, you may need to perform a number of different tasks very quickly, such as switching between application windows, editing typos in your messages and muting your microphone. By familiarising yourself with a few practical keyboard shortcuts, you will be able to multitask without wasting time and obstructing the flow of the lesson. Note that on some Apple keyboards, the 'alt' key may be labelled 'option' and 'cmd' may be labelled 'command'.

Table 1.1: Useful keyboard shortcuts	
Shortcut	*Result*
ctrl + shift + F (Windows) cmd + shift + F (Mac OS)	Sends a file via Skype.
cmd + 3 (Mac OS)	Displays your Skype contacts list.
alt + return (Mac OS)	Starts a call with the selected contact.
cmd + shift + E (Mac OS)	Edits the last message you sent.
up arrow	Edits the last message you sent if the text input field is empty.
cmd + shift + M (Mac OS)	Mutes your microphone.

Shortcut	Result
alt + tab (Windows) cmd + tab (Mac OS)	Seamlessly switches between different application windows, allowing you to quickly share different screens with the student.
ctrl + 'plus sign' (Windows) cmd + 'plus sign' (Mac OS)	Zooms in a pdf document, allowing you to enlarge text or images while sharing your screen with Skype.
alt + mute, volume up or volume down (Mac OS)	Opens your sound preferences, enabling you to select your headset for your computer's sound output.

Internet connection and data usage

A fast internet connection will ensure a better audio-visual experience and will result in fewer dropped calls. You can check the actual speed of your internet connection with a free speed test tool such as www.speedtest.net.

Table 1.2 provides Skype's recommended download and upload speeds for one-to-one calls.

Table 1.2: Skype's recommended download and upload speeds	
Call type	Download/upload speed for best performance
Calling	100Kbps/100Kbps
Video calling/screen sharing	300Kbps/300Kbps
Video calling (high quality)	500Kbps/500Kbps
Video calling (HD)	1.5Mbps/1.5Mbps

See: https://support.skype.com/en/faq/fa1417/how-much-bandwidth-does-skype-need

If you are on a limited data plan, another factor to consider is data usage. Skype's recommended connection speeds give the following data usage:

Table 1.3: Skype data usage	
Call type	*Data usage*
Calling	90MB/hour
Video calling/screen sharing	270MB/hour
Video calling (high quality)	450MB/hour
Video calling (HD)	1.35GB/hour

See: http://community.skype.com/t5/Windows-desktop-client/Video-Call-Data-Usage/td-p/706497

If you are planning to take on a full schedule of online lessons, including a high percentage of video calls, you will require a broadband internet plan that gives you unlimited data allowance. Alternatively, you may have to simply avoid video calls, unless you have regular access to a reliable and fast free Wi-Fi network.

Google Hangouts (www.google.com/hangouts/)

Google Hangouts is an increasingly popular free video chat service that can be used as an alternative to Skype. It is available to anyone with a Google account. Hangouts enables both one-to-one chats and group chats with up to 10 people at a time. The platform focuses more on 'face-to-face-to-face' group interaction as opposed to one-to-one video chats, and it utilises sophisticated technology to seamlessly switch the focus to the person currently chatting. For this reason, Google Hangouts has considerable potential for teaching a group of students simultaneously.

Google Hangouts includes some useful built-in features which make it a viable alternative to Skype. These include screen sharing and the ability to share and collaborate on a Google Doc (useful for correcting written work). Some teacher marketplaces (see Chapter 2) may be integrated with Google Hangouts, so it is a good idea to familiarise yourself with the platform.

RECORDING LESSONS AND ACTIVITIES

PrettyMay (www.prettymay.net)

PrettyMay Call Recorder for Skype (PMCRS) is a Skype extension that
enables you to record Skype calls on Windows easily (Mac users see below).
The plugin also allows you to set up an answering machine for your Skype
account, send an automatic chat reply when you are away as well as play
recorded calls and audio files during conversations. The free version
currently allows you to record up to 15 minutes of your Skype conversations.
Check the PrettyMay website for current prices.

If you are a Windows user, you will find this tool useful for playing dialogues
during the lesson as it gives you playback control and makes it possible for both
you and the student to hear the audio at the same time through your separate
speakers. In addition, the ability to record and play back lesson activities such as
roleplays can provide the student with valuable feedback. If you have just started
teaching online, you may also want to record some of your lessons, listen to your
own performance and work on any areas that need improving.

Call recorder for Skype (www.ecamm.com/mac/callrecorder/)

Call Recorder is a Skype audio and video recorder available to Mac users. Call
Recorder converts calls into Mp3 files and allows you to record video sessions
as you see them or in split-screen mode. Call Recorder is available to try for
free for a limited period (currently seven days), after which you will need to
purchase the software. Check the product website for the current price.

SHARING AND COLLABORATING

Dropbox (www.dropbox.com)

Dropbox is a popular file hosting service that allows users to create a special
folder on their computer, which Dropbox then synchronises so that it

appears to be the same folder (with the same contents) regardless of which computer is used to view it. Files placed in this folder are accessible via the folder, or through the Dropbox website and mobile app. The contents of a Dropbox folder can easily be shared with anyone by generating a link to any file or folder. This means you can instantly share materials with your students instead of using Skype's file transfer function, which can be sluggish and is not fully supported on certain devices.

Sharing materials with Dropbox is even more convenient if your students are already Dropbox members. Instead of sending links to new files, you will be able to create and maintain a shared folder for each student. Folders can be shared in this way by clicking the **Share a folder** icon in your Dropbox home screen and entering the student's email address when prompted. Non-members will be invited to register for free in order to access the folder.

Sharing folders with students who are Dropbox members has three key advantages:

- You only need to tell the student when there is a new file in the shared folder or simply rely on the automatic desktop notifications that the student should receive from Dropbox.

- A shared dialogue or podcast can be played online in the Dropbox folder, without the need to download the audio file.

- Previously shared materials can be easily accessed and viewed together with the date when each file was uploaded or modified, thus serving as an evolving course programme that gives the student a sense of progress.

A shared folder on Dropbox. (Dropbox and Dropbox logo are trademarks of Dropbox Inc. Become an Online English Teacher is not affiliated with or otherwise sponsored by Dropbox, Inc.)

A free Dropbox plan currently comes with 2GB of free space, which should be plenty if you have only a few students. Check the Dropbox website for details of their paid plans.

Google Docs (docs.google.com)

Google Docs is a free online tool that allows you to create and share documents (Docs) and spreadsheets (Sheets). Google Docs makes it possible for more than one user to edit the same file simultaneously, which is useful for correcting written work. With shared spreadsheets, you can make and share notes during the lesson in a more organised and less haphazard way than with Skype's instant messaging function. Sheets can be used to record corrected mistakes and present new vocabulary. The spreadsheet columns can be utilised to provide additional information about a word or phrase, for example its definition, common collocations, phonetic transcription, translation and examples of use. You can even insert images and links. If a language item is particularly difficult to pronounce, you could record yourself saying it, save the audio file in a Dropbox folder and insert a link to the shared file. This will allow students to click on the word or structure in the sheet itself and hear its proper pronunciation.

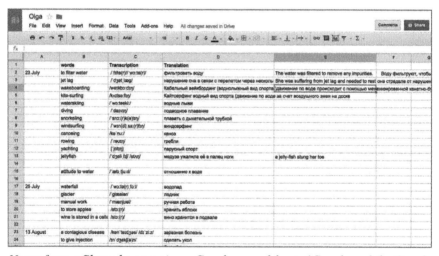

Notes from a Skype lesson using a Google spreadsheet. (Google and the Google logo are registered trademarks of Google Inc., used with permission.)

Twiddla (twiddla.com)

Twiddla is a user-friendly online whiteboard that makes it possible to share ideas and concepts in real time with other users. Anyone can be invited to view and collaborate on your whiteboard by simply sharing a URL with them. For online teachers, Twiddla can be used for a variety of purposes, including:

- drawing timelines to explain the uses of tenses
- illustrating prepositions of place
- doing collaborative lesson activities, eg. 'Circle the number that you hear.'

Not all the features may be available on every device and you will need to experiment with the tool before using it in your lessons.

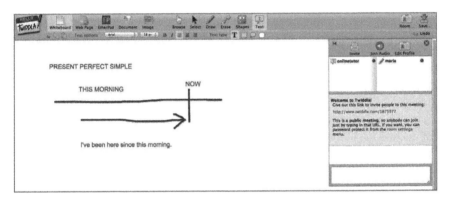

Twiddla being used to illustrate a grammatical concept. Reproduced with the kind permission of Expat Software.

COLLECTING INFORMATION

Google Forms (docs.google.com/forms/)

Google Forms is a free online tool for creating forms and collecting information from users. Google Forms enables you, as an online teacher, to create your own online needs analysis forms, level placement tests, periodic review tests and satisfaction surveys. You can choose from a variety of custom styles and question types, including multiple choice, checkboxes, text boxes and drop-down lists.

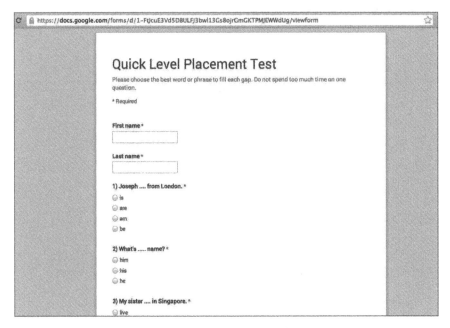

Example of a Google Form used as a level placement test. (Google and the Google logo are registered trademarks of Google Inc., used with permission.)

Information collected from a form can be displayed in a Google spreadsheet by selecting **Change response destination** from the **Responses** menu. This allows you to compare all your students' responses in one place.

Case study: creating an online test

If you want to create online tests, note that Google Forms does not currently have an option to indicate which answers are correct and automatically total scores for each respondent. However, within the Google spreadsheet where the responses are collected, you can create a formula to have the form graded. To create a self-grading test, follow the steps below.

1. Go to https://docs.google.com/forms/ and create a new form consisting of your test questions. There should be one correct answer for each question. In order to identify each respondent in the results sheet, make sure you also collect the student's name by creating an appropriate text field for the first test question.

2. Make sure you have selected a spreadsheet as the response destination from the **Responses** menu.

3. Take the test yourself in order to create a key of answers in the first row of the response spreadsheet.

4. Take the test again imagining that you are a student this time. This will ensure that you have set up everything correctly.

5. Add a final column and give it a heading, eg. 'Final score'.

6. Create a special formula that automatically generates a final test score in the 'Final score' cell for your imaginary student.

The final score formula

The final score formula is little challenging and requires you to exercise your logical brain. However, you only need to create it once and simply copy and paste it whenever a new student submits a test. So, here goes.

The formula uses an IF statement to award a point to the student IF their answer matches the answer in the key. The IF statement is formulated in the following way:

IF(CELL2=CELL1, TRUEVALUE, FALSEVALUE)

So, if the answer in CELL2 matches the answer in CELL1 (the key), then the Final score cell will give a TRUEVALUE (eg. 1 point); otherwise it will give a FALSEVALUE (eg. 0 points).

Let's imagine the test consists of one question and the student's response appears in cell C3, below the key in cell C2. The formula that you would use in the Final score cell would be:

=IF(C3=$C$2,1,0)

C3 contains the student's response, C2 contains the key, 1 represents the points awarded for a matching answer and 0 equals the points awarded for an answer that doesn't match the key. However, notice that the second cell reference includes two $ signs. Instead of C2, it is referenced as $C$2. The $ sign makes it an *absolute cell reference*, as opposed to C2, which is a *relative cell reference*.

Confused? Well, what this means is that when you copy and paste the formula into a new cell in the 'Final score' column, the cell containing the student's answer will change from C3 to C4, whereas cell C2 (the key) will always remain the same.

Since a real test consists of more than one question, we will need to calculate a final score by totalling the values of all the correct answers. For a test comprising four questions, with the key of correct answers in cells C2–F2 (row 2), the formula for calculating the final score for the imaginary student in row 3 would look like this:

=(IF(C3=$C$2,1,0)+IF(D3=$D$2,1,0)+IF(E3=$E$2,1,0)+IF(F3=$F$2,1,0))

If your imaginary student has answered each question correctly, the formula should give a perfect score. Now, whenever a new student completes a test, you simply need to copy and paste the formula into the 'Final score' cell for the new student and the total score will be displayed.

SCHEDULING SESSIONS

Google Calendar (www.google.com/calendar)

Google Calendar is a free online tool that allows you to keep track of appointments and meetings. It is available to anyone with a Google account. This tool offers a number of useful features such as the ability to share your schedule with other people, access your calendar on the go with a mobile device and receive automatic appointment reminders and notifications. Keeping a Google Calendar will greatly facilitate the appointment scheduling aspects of your work. Instead of discussing your availability at the end of each lesson, which can often be time-consuming and a little frustrating, you can simply share your calendar and let students find an available time slot.

This can currently be achieved by clicking the down-arrow button next to the appropriate calendar in your calendar list, located to the left of your calendar, and clicking **Share this calendar**. Check the option **Make this calendar public** and **Share only my free/busy information** to hide details of your appointments.

Then go back to your calendar list and select **Calendar settings**. In the **Calendar address** area, click the HTML button and you will get a public URL link which you can share with anyone who wants to view your schedule. However, you will still have to enter the appointment in your calendar yourself as the public view only allows read-only access.

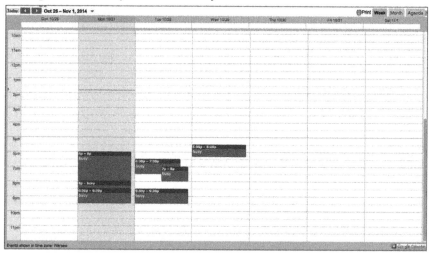

Example of a publicly shared Google Calendar. (Google and the Google logo are registered trademarks of Google Inc., used with permission.)

If you want to allow students to make changes to your schedule, click **Share this calendar**, and add the student's email address to the **Share with specific people** section, selecting an appropriate permission setting. However, the student will see details of your other appointments and the feature is only available to users who have a Google Calendar associated with their email address.

The limitations of the above method can be avoided by integrating your Google Calendar with appointment scheduling software (see below).

Appointlet (www.appointlet.com)

Appointlet is an online application that facilitates scheduling meetings with users across multiple time zones. The tool allows users to select an available time slot from an online calendar, which is configured to display your availability. If integrated with Google Calendar, available time slots will be retrieved from your Google Calendar, and when a meeting is scheduled, rescheduled or cancelled, your Google Calendar is automatically updated.

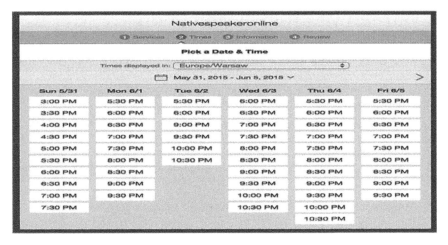

Scheduling an appointment with Appointlet

Appointlet is free if you offer only one service. Paid plans start at $9.99/month and provide additional functionality such as the ability to collect more details from appointees, offer more than one service and brand your online calendar.

Appointlet.com has a number of advantages over manually scheduling lessons or sharing your Google Calendar:

- Anyone who has your personal Appointlet URL can enter an appointment in your calendar.

- Students only see when you are available, not when you are busy.

- You can specify your working hours (Google Calendar only shows when you are busy, which does not include your sleep time!).

- Appointments can be easily cancelled or rescheduled with a click or a tap.

- You can collect useful data from the student during the scheduling process, for example their Skype username, email, country of residence, etc.

- Both you and the student receive email confirmation and reminders of appointments made, rescheduled or cancelled.

- Available time slots and scheduled appointments are always converted to each user's local time zone, eliminating any confusion and misunderstanding.

Evernote (www.evernote.com)

As an online teacher, you need an efficient system for keeping notes on your students' changing needs and for reminding yourself to get things done. Evernote is a popular application that allows you to easily make, save and share notes from a tablet, smartphone or computer. Although there are numerous other tools you could use, which include taking old-fashioned paper notes, Evernote offers a number of interesting features:

- Notes can be synchronised across different devices allowing you to access them from anywhere.

- You can clip other media to your notes, for example a recorded lesson.

- You can set reminders for particular notes, which can be useful for lesson planning and research.

- You can easily record notes instead of writing them, which you may find more convenient during a Skype lesson.

- Notes can be assigned to notebooks and tags, making it easy to retrieve information.

- Emails can be sent into Evernote, allowing you to keep a record of any relevant email correspondence with a particular student.

- If you are collaborating with another teacher, you can easily share notes.

You may need to take a variety of notes for each student, including key information from an initial needs analysis, special requests, language areas to practise, etc. If so, Evernote will allow you to establish an efficient system for collecting information. One suggested methodology is to create one notebook for all your students and make use of tags or keywords within the notes. In this way, you can use the search bar to display all notes related to a particular student by entering the student's name. You can also refine the search by entering the student's name plus a keyword or tag such as 'needs analysis' or 'exam results'.

Chapter 2:

Finding students

With an increasing number of freelance EFL tutors on the web, one of the most challenging areas for new teachers is how to attract prospective students and start filling their schedule. However, a little internet marketing know-how and a creative mindset can have a significant impact on your success.

As an online teacher, there are a number of ways you can find students. These include:

- joining an online teacher marketplace
- posting online classified ads
- contributing to forums
- creating YouTube videos
- using pay-per-click advertising
- blogging.

Each channel has its own particular advantages and disadvantages, and it is not necessary to use all the different strategies available to you. If one or two methods are working well, it is better to focus your valuable time and energy improving your results with those particular channels. This chapter will cover best practices for each strategy.

Teacher marketplaces

Teacher marketplaces are websites that act as intermediaries between online tutors and students. Each platform supplies its own appointment scheduling and payment processing system, allowing students to view teachers' availability, book online and make payments.

When it comes to payment, each model works a little differently. Some services may deduct a fixed commission from transactions for successfully completed lessons. Others may add a booking fee onto the prices set by teachers. With all platforms, you are at the mercy of the marketplace; whether you manage to fill your schedule or not may depend on your ratings, the number of students you have taught, your total completed teaching sessions and your prices in relation to other tutors.

Creating your profile

When creating your profile, study what other teachers are offering, and try to emphasise your unique selling points in relation to your competition. The following tips may help:

- Try to communicate your expertise and enthusiasm in a clear, understandable and approachable way.

- Avoid using difficult phrasal verbs and idioms in your profile description.

- Use bullet points to highlight key points if the platform enables this.

- If possible, specialise in an in-demand area where competition from other teachers is relatively low.

- If you speak any other languages, make sure you include the details.

- Include a friendly, welcoming profile image.

- Create a welcome video if the platform offers this feature (see Page 34 for video-making best practices).

In teacher marketplaces, students tend to favour teachers with the best profiles, ratings and statistics (ie. number of students and completed sessions). Some marketplaces feature popular teachers more prominently than new teachers, which means that new teachers may find it challenging to start attracting students.

Next, we will look at a few of the most popular websites, including a case study of an English teacher successfully working in a marketplace environment. Note that specific details about prices and policies refer to the time of writing and may quickly become outdated. Always check the relevant website for updated information.

italki.com

Launched in 2006, italki is popular website for language exchange and online learning. The portal has a global community of over 1,000,000 language learners and more than 1,000 language teachers, studying over 100 languages.

Teachers on italki are categorised as 'professional teachers' or 'community tutors', the former having professional teaching experience or certifications. In order to be a 'professional teacher', you need to fulfil at least one of the following criteria:

- you are a teacher by profession

- you have a university degree in education

- you have a teaching certificate, eg. CertTESOL, CELTA.

All professional teachers on italki are requested to submit their CV and upload a copy of their teaching credentials, which can be viewed on their profiles by students. Teacher profiles can also include a YouTube introduction video. In addition to providing lessons, tutors can correct other members' online written work (known as 'notebook entries'), which can help them gain exposure within the marketplace.

Both professional and community teachers are able to create a teacher profile and set their own rates for payment. italki operates a virtual currency called italki credits (ITC), which is pegged to the dollar and used to pay teachers. At the time of writing, 10 ITC = 1 USD. Credits can be converted into cash and withdrawn at any time, and italki currently charges teachers a 15% service fee for successful lesson transactions. Professional English teachers typically charge around 100–300 ITC (10–30 USD) per hour.

Verbalplanet.com

Founded in 2006, Verbalplanet is a language training and tuition service that facilitates online language classes between language learners and tutors around the globe using Skype.

To join Verbalplanet, you will need to create a tutor profile and wait for approval. Due to the increasing number of teacher applications, Verbalplanet only approve profiles that demonstrate significant language teaching experience and supporting qualifications, and it may not always be possible to apply. Check their website or Facebook page for the latest updates.

Once approved, however, you will be able set your own prices and available hours using the platform's online work planner. Many English tutors charge around $15–20 for a 45-minute session, to which Verbalplanet adds a booking fee.

Following each lesson, students are asked to leave a rating score and feedback comment. Teacher profiles with the most students and positive reviews are featured more prominently and therefore attract greater numbers of students. As a result, new teachers are encouraged to offer free trial lessons and generous loyalty discounts to attract and retain students as well as stimulate positive feedback.

www.buddyschool.com

BuddySchool.com is an online tutoring platform founded in 2007 which claims to have over 90,000 users and almost 20,000 tutors teaching more than 100 subjects. Although registration is free, there is a small fee to activate your profile (currently $1 per month, $6 per half year and $10 per year). BuddySchool takes care of lesson scheduling and operates a credit system for payments.

www.testedteachers.com

Founded in 2012–2013, testedteachers.com is a Swiss-based teacher marketplace that 'makes sure their teachers can teach'. Teachers can register for free, although there is an application process which involves a Skype-based interview. Like other marketplaces, testedteachers.com handles lesson scheduling and payment. The service's commission depends on how many lessons the teacher gives. (Exact figures are not published on the website.) According to a customer service representative interviewed on the subject, the lowest figure is 16.5% at the time of publication, which is easily obtainable according to the company. Teachers' earnings are paid out by PayPal on the first of every month. Testedteachers.com also offers full-time customer service to help members with any problems or booking issues.

Case study: italki

Former online tutor Austin Wood has the following advice for making money on italki.

'Start your prices low, especially while you don't have any stats/reviews. I started at $10/hour then bumped it up by $1–2 every time I reached 50% of max capacity (that is, if I have 10 hours available per week to teach and I'm consistently filling up five of those hours).

When you raise your prices, avoid alienating your loyal clients until you've reached that next 50% max capacity. You can do this by creating packages with discounts. Write them a message saying you're raising your prices, but until *such date* you'd like to continue providing them your old price via the five-lesson package. Of course, don't bother doing this for clients who you're sure will pay your new price!

When I was actively searching for clients and still had few stats, I made corrections to at least one random notebook entry every day. This increases your visibility, not only in searches, but people can also just find you by browsing notebook entries.

It's possible to add an introduction video. I never did this (I don't think the option was available when I started teaching), but it's probably a very good idea. Many students are skeptical that the teacher is a native speaker, or are worried that the lesson will start and they won't understand a word the teacher says. If they can watch a short intro video, this will help remove their skepticism and insecurity.

Reply to session requests and messages as quickly as possible. In my experience this increases trust. I always logged in at least once every 24 hours and responded to everything.

Specialize (especially after you have some stats). TOEFL prep is a great example of this. On italki, I specialized in TOEFL preparation, maths and physics tutoring and beginner/pre-intermediate English for native Russian speakers. For now, I'd recommend keeping TOEFL at $15 and taking your conversation down to $10. At the end of my Skype career, I had about 10 hours per week of "specialized" lessons at $18–20/hour and another 10–15 hours per week of conversation at $16. It's probably pretty difficult to raise prices much more than that on italki, just because students have so many options available to them. I experimented with finding clients outside of italki and picked up a few at $25/hour, but the scheduling and advertising that italki offers is probably worth the lower wages.

Consider recording and watching your lessons (I use Call Recorder for Mac). Obviously don't waste time doing this for every lesson, but I did this quite frequently at the beginning and often noticed things I could do better and would actively try and improve during my next lesson. italki students often have experience with many teachers, so they'll be able

> to recognise a good teacher when they meet one. Always focus on improving your teaching abilities and increase your fee accordingly.'
>
> *Reproduced with the kind permission of Austin Wood (www.austin.bio).*

Although Austin was a member of italki, much of his advice can be considered relevant to teachers looking for students in other marketplace platforms.

Final thoughts

Teacher marketplaces clearly offer useful benefits. The commission fees charged are a small price to pay for free promotion, payment processing, lesson scheduling and other administrative issues that the platforms typically handle for you. However, marketplaces will always be governed by the forces of demand and supply. With their growing popularity among teachers, it may become increasingly challenging for new tutors to establish a reputation, charge adequate prices and start attracting students.

The rest of this chapter will cover marketing strategies for online tutors who wish to go it alone, although they can be used to promote a marketplace profile as well. Just remember that if you have the ability to charge students independently (see Chapter 6), you must not attempt to circumvent any marketplace's commission or booking fees by making private arrangements with students. This is both unprofessional and could result in the closure of your account. Always read the website's terms and conditions.

Posting online classified ads

Classified advertising is one of the oldest marketing channels used by freelance teachers, predating the internet age. When online classifieds emerged, teachers quickly took advantage of the new medium and began posting ads for their tuition services. The first online teachers may have offered face-to-face tuition in this way and then branched out into online teaching to meet demand.

Posting a classified is usually free, although you may have to pay to boost your ad's exposure within the marketplace. Depending on the website, there may also be restrictions on posting an ad if you are not physically located in the same region that you are targeting, or if your advertising text is in another language. Unlike online teacher marketplaces, classified websites do not provide payment processing and scheduling tools, so you will need to handle your own billing, scheduling and workflow.

Creating your ad

Strictly speaking, classifieds cater for local services, and most students browsing the marketplace are looking for a face-to-face teacher. However, the following tips may help you attract online students:

- Focus on a city or region where there may be a shortage of available local teachers with your unique skills or background.

- Try to make your ad somehow relevant to the region you are targeting, eg. by translating the text, promoting the fact that you speak the local language (if you do), or somehow referring to the region itself in the ad copy.

- Try to 'sell' the benefits of online learning in your ad and reassure the potential student that it can be just as effective, if not more effective, than face-to-face tuition.

As with teacher marketplaces, it is important to study the competition. If there are other online teachers posting in the same region, what makes you different? Try to emphasise one or more unique selling points in relation to the others. In particular, try to find a need that is not being catered for.

Some examples:

- You are a native or proficient speaker of English that speaks the local language of the region you are targeting.

- You have 10 years' teaching experience.

- You offer a free trial lesson.

- You have a background in business.

- You specialise in a particular area, eg. IELTS/TOEFL preparation.

Here are some additional tips for generating interest in your advert:

- Keep the title short, snappy and to the point.

- Ensure that your advert is long enough to include details of your methods, experience and qualifications.

- Create a happy, humorous and approachable impression throughout the advert text.

- Don't post the same advert too many times as this may result in people regarding you as a spammer and being reluctant to engage with you.

- Use a good quality photograph of yourself to reassure viewers that you are a real person.

- Include short quotes from some of your recent students' testimonials as this can give add credence to your advert, and link through to the full version on your website or LinkedIn page so it's clear the students are real.

Of all the different marketing channels available to you, posting a classified ad is probably the most challenging in terms of building credibility. This can be mitigated, however, by including a link to your website or blog, if you have one. The importance of credibility will be discussed throughout the marketing sections of this book.

Search engine optimisation (SEO)

Depending on the local competition as well as factors specific to the classifieds site itself, the webpage displaying your advert may also achieve a high position in Google's search engine rankings for local users. This will increase your exposure beyond the classifieds community and lead to more interest. In order to maximise this serendipitous effect, make sure it is clear what you are offering in the title and body of your ad, and include words that a student would use when searching for an online tutor. If you are posting on more than one website, make sure that you create unique content for each advert – Google and other search engines consider duplicated content as spam and will not display your page at the top of their rankings.

Where to post

Research your country's online classifieds market and try to find a few suitable websites to post on. Some sites may even focus specifically on private tuition and enable student reviews.

The most popular classified ad networks are described next.

Gumtree

Founded in 2000, Gumtree.com is an online classifieds and community website. Classified ads are either free or paid for depending on the product category and the geographical market. Gumtree is now the largest classified ads site in the UK, Australia, South Africa and Singapore. In the UK alone, the website receives 14.8 million monthly unique visitors, according to a traffic audit conducted in November 2010. At the time of writing, Gumtree operates in the following countries:

United Kingdom (www.gumtree.com)

Ireland (www.gumtree.ie)

Poland (www.gumtree.pl)

Australia (www.gumtree.com.au)

South Africa (www.gumtree.co.za)

Singapore (http://singapore.gumtree.sg/)

Kijiji

Launched in 2005, Kijiji is a network of classified ads sites available for more than 110 communities in the following countries and regions:

Canada (www.kijiji.ca)

Italy (www.kijiji.it)

According to site's owner – the eBay Classifieds Group – Kijiji attracts nearly 200 million monthly visits and is the most popular online classifieds service in Canada.

Craigslist

Craigslist (www.craigslist.org) is a classified ads website and network that was founded in 1995 in San Francisco. It now covers over 700 cities in 70 countries and is available in non-English languages including Spanish, French, Italian, German and Portuguese. Despite its archaic design aesthetic, the site serves over 20 billion page views per month, putting it in 37th place overall among websites worldwide.

Every country-specific Craigslist website has its own domain name extension. To find a local Craigslist, enter 'Craigslist + [NAME OF COUNTRY OR CITY]' in Google.

Final thoughts

With the existence of teacher marketplaces, posting a classified ad seems an outdated method of finding online students. However, this does not mean that you cannot make classifieds work for you. As with all marketing strategies, the only way to find out is to test and compare your results with other approaches.

Commenting on forums

Another way you can reach new students is by posting comments on EFL learner forums. This can work well if the forum allows you to include a link in the signature of your posts or on your profile page. You can link to your website, if you have one, or some other online profile where you are offering lessons. Make sure it is clear in the signature and in your profile that you are an online teacher.

In order to make the most out of this strategy, try to follow the best practices and tips below.

- Take some time to study the forum, read the guidelines and get to know its unique culture before you start contributing.

- Don't include a signature too early. Wait until you've started to build a reputation, otherwise members might assume you are there to market and could be reluctant to open up to you.

- Make sure your comments are genuinely helpful. Contribute value and let your knowledge as a native or fluent English speaker speak for itself.

- Don't ever try to sell your tuition service blatantly or come across as a spammer. This includes sending private messages to promote your lessons to forum members.

- Try to comment regularly on the same forum and become an active member of the community.

- If you have a blog, link to a post on your site that adds further clarity to a particular problem. However, avoid doing this until you have the trust and respect of the community and make sure you are not infringing the forum guidelines.

In addition to the exposure to other members of the forum, your comments may appear in search engine results pages for queries related to topic of the forum thread.

Where to comment

When researching forums, look for indicators of popularity such as the number of views and replies that posts typically receive. If you specialise in a particular area, for example IELTS or TOEFL preparation, try to find forums that cater specifically for your target market or which include popular categories relevant to your niche.

Here is a sample of EFL forums you might consider:

UsingEnglish.com
UsingEnglish features a number of learner forum categories, including Ask a Teacher, designed for learners to ask teachers questions about the English language.

EnglishClub.com
EnglishClub includes a forum in which EFL teachers can help learners with their language problems. Popular forum category topics include grammar help, vocabulary help and writing help.

ieltsnetwork.com
IELTS Network is a popular forum for IELTS test candidates and instructors.

YouTube marketing

Online video is an extremely effective medium for gaining exposure, showcasing your expertise and establishing yourself as an authority in your field. YouTube, the most popular channel for sharing video content, allows you to freely publish videos and create your own channel. Some online teachers are so successful on YouTube that they can rely on this platform alone for acquiring students.

Video making

Creating effective videos, however, is initially time-consuming and requires a little investment. However, it is certainly possible to minimise your expenses.

Best practices for recording video:

- Keep the lighting bright and balanced using home lamps or a softbox lighting kit.

A softbox lighting kit

- Use a quality microphone for recording audio – good audio is more important than good video, and if you are going to invest in equipment, you should purchase a decent microphone (for example, a clip-on wireless Lavalier mic) before investing in a quality camera.

- Use your smartphone if you don't have a suitable digital camera such as a DSLR. Most modern smartphones can record in high resolution 720p, and tripod mount holders for mobile devices are inexpensive.

- Have a clean, contrasting and well-lit background.

- Aim for 5–10 minutes video length.

- Do a free trial of any video-editing software you intend to use.

- Speak directly to the camera as though it were a person and try to convey confidence and enthusiasm.

YouTube tips

There is a great deal of free YouTube marketing advice available on the web. Here are a few general tips:

- In your video title and description, try to include words that users would enter in YouTube's search bar to find your video.

- In the video description, include a link to your website or blog (if you have one) or to an online profile where you offer lessons.

- Keep the concept of the videos simple, eg. a whiteboard presentation of a learner's problem or some tips for succeeding in a particular exam.

- Include a call to action at the end of your videos, eg. invite your viewers to subscribe to your channel or visit your blog.

- Don't try to sell your lessons in every video.

- Include a sales video promoting your lessons as your channel trailer.

Final thoughts

If you aren't camera shy, video marketing is a highly effective promotional strategy. With a popular channel on YouTube, potential students will trust you and be willing to engage with you. In addition, popular videos are featured more prominently in YouTube's search results and also in Google's organic search results pages. At the end of this chapter, you will find some links to helpful video-making tools and resources.

Pay-per-click advertising

Pay-per-click (PPC) advertising is a very common internet advertising model in which the advertiser is charged when an ad is clicked on. In contrast to the strategies outlined in this chapter so far, you cannot use this form of advertising without owning a website. Although PPC adverts can drive a lot of traffic to your site, that traffic literally comes at a price, and your success depends on whether you can attract enough new students and achieve a return on your investment. It is therefore the most risky strategy and generally not recommended unless you know what you are doing.

Next, we will look at two widely used advertising platforms that operate PPC ads:

- Google Adwords

- Facebook Adverts.

Google Adwords (www.adwords.com)

With Google Adwords, advertisers 'bid' on words and phrases that potential clients might be searching for. Maximum bids are either set by the advertiser or they can be automatically set by Adwords. A user searching for a term you are bidding on, eg. 'learn English on Skype', will trigger your ad to be displayed next to or above the organic search results – as long as your maximum bid is high enough and you haven't excluded the user's geographic region in your campaign settings.

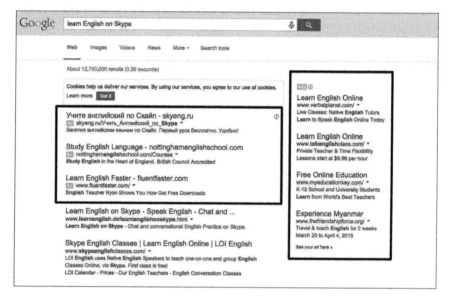

A Google search results page with PPC adverts highlighted. (Google and the Google logo are registered trademarks of Google Inc., used with permission.)

Every time your ad is clicked on, Google charges your account. The actual amount that you pay per click (the 'cost per click' or CPC) is calculated by the Adwords system and depends on a number of factors, including the level of competition and the relevance of your webpage and advert to the term you are bidding for. Your maximum bid, if you have set one, caps the amount that you are willing to pay but may significantly reduce your ad's exposure if set too low.

If you have a well-performing ad (an ad that attracts a relatively high number of clicks) together with a well-optimised 'landing page' (the page that users are taken to when they click on your ad), Google Adwords rewards you with a lower CPC. If you follow the best practices described in Chapter 3 for creating your tuition promotion page, you should have a well-performing landing page. However, you may want to build additional landing pages for more specialised services tailored to more specific adverts, eg. business English or TOEFL preparation. Within your Adwords account, you would need to create separate ad groups and target keywords.

Facebook Adverts (facebook.com/business/marketing/facebook)

Facebook operates a highly targeted advertising model which allows you to precisely define your target audience among the network's user base and create an ad that will be displayed in their News Feed. When it comes to cost, you can choose between two models:

- cost per thousand impressions or CPM (M stands for 'thousand' in Latin)
- cost per click or CPC.

You can create ads that link to your landing page and include a 'Like' button enabling viewers to like your Facebook page, if you have one. When adverts are liked, shared or commented on, friends of the target audience member may see the advert, which increases the effectiveness of the ad.

What distinguishes Facebook's advertising model is the extent to which you can define your audience. You can select your audience by interests (learning English, preparing for FCE, business English, etc.), geographic region, age, gender, education, field of work, etc. If you offer a specialised tuition service, these filters can help you reach a very specific target audience.

Conclusions

Google Adwords, Facebook Adverts and other similar platforms can be extremely complex, and explaining the different features and optimisation strategies is beyond the scope of this book. The further reading section at the end of this chapter includes some resources to help you get started. If you can consistently achieve a return on your investment and convert new students into loyal customers, then you will find PPC advertising to be a very reliable and generally hands-off marketing channel. However, this is by no means guaranteed, and online teachers tend to have mixed results with the system.

Blogging

Blogging is a highly effective long-term marketing activity. This strategy enables you to establish a reputation within your field and increase your exposure over time through online search and social-media sharing, as well as via links from forums and other blogs. In contrast to a teacher marketplace, where there are many tutors competing for the same students, visitors to your website will not have that luxury of choice. Additionally, you are not at the mercy of reviews and statistics. Maintaining a blog does require regular writing, but if you are enjoying it, this won't feel like hard work.

Building a blog from scratch may at first seem daunting to some teachers, but fortunately there are a number of free tools and open-source platforms (dealt with in the next chapter) which you can use to develop your site without the need for coding skills. It is also important to note that any initial learning curve will be greatly outweighed by the long-term benefits.

Content for blog posts

If you are teaching regularly, whether online or face-to-face, your students will provide the inspiration for many of your blog posts. During your lessons, make notes of typical areas that your students are having problems with and try to think how you can help other learners understand them better. Perhaps you can illustrate your point with a simple anecdote or a picture. Also, remember that you don't always need to create your own content. For example, you can embed other people's YouTube videos in your posts.

The more you enjoy your writing, the more you will be inspired to write. Here are some examples of ideas for your posts:

- Clarify the difference between two or more confusing words.
- Explain an idiom or phrasal verb.
- Create an infographic to illustrate a difficult concept.
- Review a website or product that your potential students may be interested in.
- Publish some tips for exam takers.
- Embed a useful YouTube video and include your own commentary.

Here are some additional general blogging tips:

- Establish a posting schedule (once a day, three times a week, etc.) and stick to it.
- Include feature images for your posts (see Chapter 3).
- Give examples to support explanations or definitions.
- Double-check the information in your posts by researching online.
- Keep your language clear and accessible.
- Include humour where appropriate, eg. pictures of amusing mistranslations.
- Try to come up with your own unique perspective and style.
- Include a regular feature, eg. Whiteboard Wednesday or Idiom of the Day.
- Translate your posts if you are targeting a particular nationality.

Conclusion

Blogging as a means to attract new students requires some patience, and it has a cumulative effect: the more mature your website, the greater the return on your effort. However, a blog can also be used to enhance the effectiveness of all the other marketing strategies mentioned in this chapter simply by increasing your credibility. The next few chapters will explain how to set up and promote your blog.

Final thoughts

If you are new to online teaching, there is no magic button that will instantly fill your schedule with new students. Due to the competitive nature of the online tutoring space, you need to 'think smart', and the marketing tactics that you decide to use will largely depend on your goals. Your best approach might simply be to target a group of learners with specialised needs, or a specific geographic market that isn't being fully catered for. If your goal is to reach students from anywhere in the world or to charge as much as possible for a lesson, then the strategies designed to enhance your credibility and reputation will be more important. If you are looking for a relatively hands-off approach and just want to gain some experience then you might try your luck in a teacher marketplace or post online classified ads, at the same time offering a free trial lesson and/or relatively low prices.

Table 2.1 summarises the different marketing options covered in this chapter.

Table 2.1: Marketing options		
	Pros	*Cons*
Teacher marketplace	■ Free to join pending approval ■ Handles payment processing and scheduling ■ Easy to create a profile ■ Gives you access to students looking for online tuition	■ If you lack experience or qualifications, you may not get approval ■ Could be challenging for new tutors to establish a reputation and gain enough exposure within the marketplace ■ Charges commission fees
Classifieds	■ Typically no approval process or waiting period ■ Ads are free or relatively inexpensive ■ Can help you target a specific region	■ Difficult to establish credibility in the absence of reviews and ratings ■ Competition can be stiff ■ Exposure is limited to a local market
Forums	■ Free to join ■ Posting is usually quick and easy ■ Possible to target a specific community	■ Requires frequent contributions to be effective
YouTube	■ Very effective for building a reputation ■ Potential for videos to be shared and reach a wide audience ■ Potential for videos to be positioned highly in Google search results pages	■ Requires some initial investment ■ Making videos, using video editing software and uploading video files can be time consuming

	Pros	Cons
PPC	■ Drives traffic to a website almost immediately ■ Target audience can be highly refined	■ It can be difficult to achieve a return on investment ■ Can be very expensive if budget is not tightly controlled
Blogging	■ Builds credibility and reputation over time ■ Increases exposure in search engine results ■ Potential for posts to be shared ■ Enhances other marketing strategies	■ Initial learning curve ■ Requires regular writing

Further resources

Video creation

Video-editing software

The following editing tools are free and include basic editing features:

■ Windows Movie Maker (for Windows)

■ iMovie (for Mac).

The following user-friendly tools are relatively inexpensive and provide more professional editing features as well as screen capture:

■ Camtasia (for Windows and Mac) http://www.techsmith.com/camtasia.html

■ Screenflow (for Mac) http://www.telestream.net/screenflow/overview.htm

The following tools are for more professional video-making:

- Adobe Premiere http://www.adobe.com/products/premiere.html
- Final Cut Pro (for Mac) http://www.apple.com/final-cut-pro/

Video-making tips

https://vimeo.com/videoschool/101

http://wistia.com/learning/video-production

https://www.teachertrainingvideos.com/

Marketing

YouTube marketing tips

https://www.youtube.com/yt/playbook/channel-optimization.html

https://blog.kissmetrics.com/2013-youtube-marketing-guide/

Google/Facebook advertising

http://offers.hubspot.com/marketing-ebook/introductory-guide-to-paid-search

http://www.wordstream.com/category/wordstream-blog-tags/adwords-tips

https://www.facebook.com/business/a/campaign-structure

Blog creation

Blogging tips

The following websites feature online blogging tips as well as free downloadable e-books on blogging-related topics:

http://www.copyblogger.com/blog/

http://blog.hubspot.com/marketing/topic/blogging

Blogging resources

These websites include images that you may be able to use in your blog posts for free (with the correct attribution):

http://search.creativecommons.org/

www.wikipedia.org

These online photo libraries allow you to purchase royalty-free photos:

www.dreamstime.com

www.istockphoto.com

Use this tool to create your own free infographics:

www.easel.ly

Chapter 3:

Building a blog

In Chapter 2, we compared teaching through an online marketplace and going it alone. Going it alone and having a professional-looking website for your business can help you increase your credibility; it can also provide a number of other useful benefits:

- you can potentially charge a higher price for your lessons
- you are not competing with other teachers on the same platform
- you are not at the mercy of reviews and statistics
- you keep 100% of your lesson fees (minus any payment processing charges)
- you can develop valuable web skills that may come in handy should you outgrow online teaching.

A website with blogging functionality (which we will call a blog) allows you to increase your exposure through regular posting, as explained in Chapter 2. In this chapter, you will learn how to build your own English language learning blog from scratch without the need for any coding.

Site-building tools

There are an increasing number of free tools and open source platforms you can use to design your website. Some platforms offer free blog building tools and hosting (free hosted blogs) while others enable you to install their platform on your own domain and hosting account (self-hosted blogs). With WordPress, the world's most popular blogging platform, both options are available.

Free hosted blogs

The cheapest and easiest way to get started is to use a free website builder and hosting service such as Weebly, Wix, Blogger or WordPress.

Signing up for a free hosted blog is usually very quick; it typically involves entering the title you have chosen for your blog, your email address, a password and then selecting one of the available themes.

Although they are called 'free blogs', it is important to note that most of these tools offer paid plans allowing you to use more advanced features and/or get additional storage space. Free plans may also display text ads on your site.

Next, we will look at the two popular types of hosted service: drag-and-drop website builders and hosted blogging platforms.

Drag-and-drop builders

Website builders such as Weebly (www.weebly.com) and Wix (www.wix. com) feature a drag-and-drop interface that allows you to build a website in editing mode as you would see it published. For this reason, they are the easiest and most intuitive tools to use.

These platforms enable you to easily add a variety of basic building elements to your pages such as paragraphs, titles, images, buttons, contact forms, videos, maps and social media. They even give you the ability to integrate appointment scheduling, which is particularly useful to online language tutors. Although not usually classed as 'blogging platforms', these website builders do include the ability to publish posts with the click of a button. Once published, users can comment on posts and share them on social media.

Building a web page with Weebly.

Hosted blogging platforms

The most popular hosted blogging platforms on the web are Blogger (Blogspot.com) and WordPress.com. Blogger is owned by Google, and you need a Google account to use it. It is a completely free model with no restrictions. With WordPress.com, you need to sign up with an email address, username and password. The free plan comes with limited features, and if you need more than 3GB of space, you will need to upgrade.

Both Blogger and WordPress offer a compartmentalised dashboard for building your site. Instead of a drag-and-drop interface, these platforms feature a toolbar which allows you to add posts, pages and widgets to your site.

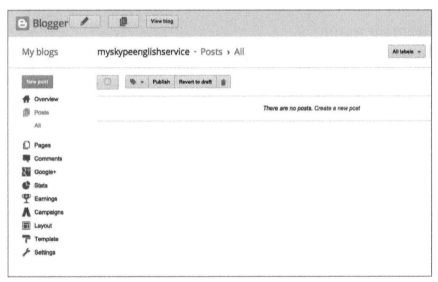

The Blogger dashboard. (Google and the Google logo are registered trademarks of Google Inc., used with permission.)

Posts are the actual pages of your blog. Depending on your chosen design template, posts are usually displayed on the blog's front page in the order that they are published, although you can configure another page for your blog.

Pages are for timeless content that you want to be easily accessible, for example your 'About' or 'Contact' pages. In contrast to posts, pages are not always automatically displayed on the front end of your site, so you would need to link to them manually via a menu or within a post. Many theme designs include a standard 'About' page that is accessible from the main header menu.

Widgets (also known as 'gadgets') are small blocks of content or functionality that you usually add to the sidebar of your website. Examples of widgets include Facebook-like boxes and simple email sign-up forms.

In order to see what a post or page looks like before publishing, you would need to click the **Preview** button.

Despite their slightly steeper learning curve, Blogger and WordPress offer more blogging features than the drag-and-drop editors. WordPress in particular includes access to hundreds of free themes. If you intend to translate your content for a particular market, make sure 'Translation Ready' is included in your WordPress theme's list of features.

Domain name

When creating a free hosted blog, you will need to choose a name for your site and decide whether to go with a free subdomain, eg. example.weebly.com, example.blogspot.com, example.wordpress.com, or pay a modest annual fee for your own custom domain, eg. example.com. Although you can certainly attract students with a subdomain, having your own domain obviously looks more professional and generally indicates that you are serious about your business.

Self-hosted blogs

For self-hosted blogs, WordPress provides a different resource site – WordPress.org. Building a self-hosted WordPress blog involves the steepest learning curve and incurs regular hosting and domain registration fees. However, this type of blog offers several significant advantages:

- you can choose from a vast number of free and commercial themes

- you can upload any free or paid plugin from WordPress.org (see page 49), which allows you to add almost any kind of functionality you want

- there are no storage limits except those imposed by your hosting plan (and many affordable plans offer unrestricted storage).

To set up a self-hosted WordPress blog, you first need to purchase a domain name and a shared hosting package from a reputable hosting company. Popular hosts such as HostGator (www.hostgator.com) offer unlimited storage plans for a modest recurring fee. You will also need to ensure that the hosting service provides a user-friendly admin panel such as cPanel, which will allow you to install WordPress with one click.

Hostgator's user-friendly admin panel.

Readers of *Become an Online English Teacher: Essential tools, strategies and methodologies for building a successful business* are entitled to a 25% discount on HostGator's web hosting plans using the coupon code TEACHINGONLINE25.

Once you have installed WordPress, you will be able to choose from a vast number of free and commercial themes to replace your site's default theme. Themes come with pre-installed added features such as a contact form, spam filter, search box, etc. These are called 'plugins'. There is a plethora of additional free and paid plugins to choose from at WordPress.org. Some of these plugins may enhance your online teaching service and allow you more room for creativity with your marketing efforts.

Both free and self-hosted WordPress blogs come with a versatile editing tool that allows you to easily include text, hyperlinks, images, audio and snippets of code in any page or post.

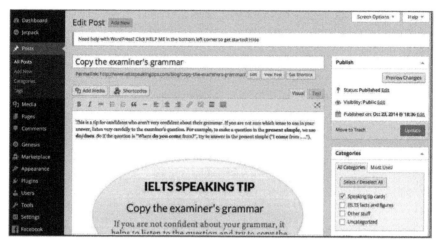

Creating a post with WordPress.

By default, WordPress blogs do not come with an intuitive front-end drag-and-drop editor as Weebly or Wix do. From time to time, you may want to make certain adjustments to the layout of a page template, for example, adding extra columns or blocks of elements. In WordPress, this can be quite difficult to achieve without the hired help of a WordPress professional. Fortunately, however, there has been a recent development in so-called 'page builder' plugins which allow you to build self-hosted WordPress pages using a drag-and-drop interface. These tools take the pain out of building pages and give you more control over the look and feel of your website. One such page builder is recommended in the resource section of this chapter.

WordPress is an extremely powerful content management system, and it is beyond the scope of this book to describe every feature of this platform. However, the further resources section at the end of this chapter includes links to WordPress documentation and tutorials to help you get started.

Final thoughts

If you have decided to build a website or blog, there are a great number of free or relatively inexpensive tools. Your choice of platform should be determined by your goals and whether you are prepared to take the time to learn a new skill. If you just want to painlessly create a simple, elegant website with basic blogging features, then a drag-and-drop editor such as Weebly should suffice. If you want a free tool with more robust blogging features, and provided you don't mind a slight learning curve, then go with

Blogger or hosted WordPress.com. If you want the flexibility to customise your site in whatever way you like and you are prepared to invest in hosting fees and domain registration, then a self-hosted WordPress blog is the recommended choice.

Below is a summary of the different options. This is by no means an exhaustive list of the differences between each platform. The resources section at the end of this chapter provides links to further information.

Table 3.1: Pros and cons of different platforms

	Pros	Cons
Weebly	■ Very easy and intuitive for beginners ■ Comes with hosting ■ Good blogging feature ■ Offers personal support	■ Limited blogging features compared to Blogger and WordPress ■ Certain useful features only come with a paid plan
Blogger	■ Reliable hosting (hosted on Google's servers) ■ 100% free ■ Signing up is effortless if you already have a Google account ■ Very good blogging platform	■ Steeper learning curve than Weebly ■ Although you can create unlimited posts, there may be limits on the number of pages you can create (currently 20)
WordPress.com	■ High number of available free themes ■ Very good blogging platform ■ Easy to set up ■ Free if you have a blog with basic features ■ Offers personal support	■ Steeper learning curve than Weebly ■ Not all features are free ■ Not allowed to upload any plugins (the platform comes with its own built-in plugin features) ■ No-ads upgrade costs $30/year

	Pros	Cons
Self-hosted WordPress	■ Vast number of themes and plugins to choose from ■ Extensive support community ■ The most robust and feature-rich blogging platform	■ Steeper learning curve ■ You need to pay for your own web hosting and domain registration (which professional bloggers would actually consider a plus) ■ You may need to hire a WordPress developer if you want to make complex adjustments to page layouts (unless you install a page builder plugin)

Choosing a theme

Whatever platform you use to build your site, the design aesthetic is important. Your template or theme should have both a personal and professional look and feel. One problem with websites built with online tools is that they begin to look generic since the platforms are so widespread. In addition, many of the themes provided are tailored to corporate websites and often feature design fads such as large image slideshows.

As a freelance online tutor, you are probably more likely to attract students with a simple, elegant theme. If possible, choose a mobile responsive template – where the page layout changes to suit different screen sizes or browser windows. This will ensure a good user experience on different devices and improve your site's ranking in mobile searches. One of the advantages of a self-hosted WordPress blog is the vast number of free and paid themes to choose from. Installing a page builder plugin with your WordPress blog (see the resources section) can help you further customise the look and feel of your pages.

Try to avoid corporate style templates – themes that typically include full-sized images or slideshows and which look and feel as though they represent a large business. This type of template will send out confusing signals to prospective students, and corporations are often associated with higher prices, impersonal customer service and bureaucracy. Your selling point is that you are an approachable, independent tutor dedicated to helping learners improve their English. This asset should be reflected in the design of your website.

Your website name

Whether you choose a subdomain or a regular domain name for your site, make it easy to remember. Limit it to six syllables or fewer and try to include a keyword such as 'English'. This may help potential students find your site in Google's search engine rankings. Examples of keyword enhanced names include englishtutoronline, learnenglishwithpaul, craigsenglishstudio, etc.

Should you decide to purchase a domain name, think about your target market. If you want to attract students from all around the world, go with a dot com (.com) domain name if available. Apart from being the most recognised extension, most internet users will type '.com' into their browsers after the name of the brand they are looking for. It is also argued that search engines favour .com websites in their results pages for searches whose relevance is not restricted to a specific geographical area.

Targeting the whole world means potential exposure to a considerable number of students. However, there may be good reasons to focus on a single country, for example, if you are not a native speaker of English or if you are a native speaker but you speak the language of a particular country fluently. The competition will be significantly less intense, and if you choose a foreign language website name together with a specific country domain extension (eg. .fr for France), your website is likely to be more visible in local foreign language searches without great effort on your part.

Search engine optimisation is covered in more detail in the next chapter.

Your business page(s)

You will need one or more pages where you present yourself and your services, and enable prospective students to contact you. These pages are fundamental to the success of your business. They should be easily accessible from every other page on your website and have a single goal – to get your visitors to take action, for example, request a trial lesson/consultation, contact you or make a payment.

The five-second test

The design and layout of the page is extremely important. A visitor should be able to determine within five seconds exactly what you are offering and what action needs to be taken next. Take a look at the design of profile pages in the teacher marketplace websites mentioned in Chapter 2. These pages have been designed by professionals with the single aim of converting visitors into paying students.

Apply the principles below, making full use of your template's sidebar or column structure, and you will have a well-optimised business page.

Get to the point and avoid clutter

First-time visitors do not typically read through an entire webpage of text as if it were the first page of a novel. They will normally scan a page to find what they are looking for. Try to follow the tips below:

- Give the page an actionable title, such as 'Book an Online English Lesson' or 'Take a Skype English Lesson'.
- Be as concise as possible.
- Use clear headers and sub headers.
- Include easy-to-scan bullet points.
- Emphasise key points with bold text.
- Utilise white space on the page to make your key points stand out and avoid clutter.
- Don't overuse images and video.

Keep the language simple

It is common sense that if you are going to craft your message in English, your language should be as comprehensible as possible to learners. Avoid phrasal verbs, complex grammatical structures and idiomatic expressions. If you intend to target potential students in their native language, then you obviously won't need to simplify as much. However, try to keep the message personal and professional at the same time. Your personality and expertise should shine through your writing.

Include an image or video

A high-quality, friendly photo of yourself will make your page more credible and encourage students to engage with you. Some successful online teachers have even used pictures of themselves enjoying a hobby. This adds a personal touch and helps to build a greater sense of trust. However, you should also think about the image you would like to convey to your target market. If you are exclusively targeting law firms, for example, you might want to be photographed in more formal attire.

In addition to your photo, consider embedding a welcome video (see Chapter 2 for best practices). Speaking directly to the student on camera will give your credibility an added boost.

Include testimonials

A few testimonials from satisfied learners will help build additional trust among your prospective students. If you don't have any written testimonials, think of what your students have said about you and ask their permission to post their quotes on your site together with the student's first name and country of origin underneath. Obviously the more information you can give about a student, the more effective the testimonial. Ideally, you would want to provide the student's photo, full name and profession if relevant.

Mention any other languages that you speak

Some lower-level students are specifically looking for teachers who can speak their native language. Presenting your linguistic abilities will help to make your services more appealing to them.

Include a brief biography

Include some information about your background, qualifications, expertise and experience.

Include scanned certificates (optional)

Do you hold any certificates in English language teaching (CertTESOL, CELTA, etc.)? Consider scanning and including them on your page. This will reassure potential students that you are qualified to teach them and will justify charging higher fees for your lessons.

Include a call to action

What action do you want a prospective student to take after reading your page? If you would like them to request a trial lesson, contact you or purchase a lesson package, include a clear instruction at the end of the description of your service or in the sidebar of your page. Use a button or large font to make the call to action stand out. If you are using an appointment scheduling tool (see Chapter 1), you can link your call-to-action message to your online schedule, enabling students to book a trial lesson or consultation with a few clicks.

Publish your prices

Even if you are offering a free trial lesson or consultation, you should make it clear that there is a price for your service and let your visitors know how much it costs. Responding to enquiries from uninformed students can be time-consuming and frustrating. Display a table or link to a page showing the different prices of your lesson packages (see Chapter 2).

Include a contact form

If you want to encourage prospective students to contact you, it is essential that you include a contact form. The form should contain the following fields: Name, Email, Skype (optional), Location, Message.

The visitor's location is very important as this will help you schedule an online appointment taking into account the time zone difference. It may also give you an early indication of how likely it is that the prospective student will become a paying student – you will probably experience more success with some regions than others.

If you have a self-hosted blog, consult the contact form documentation for customising the different fields. If you are using a free WordPress.com blog, you can easily create a contact form from the page editor. Finally, don't forget to test the form!

Include a Skype chat button (optional)

You can also enable prospective clients to get in touch with you instantly by including a Skype chat button, which you can generate here:

http://www.skype.com/en/features/skype-buttons/create-skype-buttons/

Simply select the functionality you require and copy and paste the generated code into your webpage, where you would like it to appear. In order to add code to a webpage, consult the support documentation of your website builder. In many cases this will simply involve adding an HTML 'embed' code element or widget to your page.

You can choose whether you want users to call you or whether you would rather they start the conversation with an instant message. If you don't want to answer voice calls, select the option 'Start the conversation with an instant message'. Once you have added the button to your page, you may need to change your Skype privacy settings to allow anyone to contact you.

Include PayPal buttons

Including a PayPal button on your website will make it easier for clients to purchase your service and also looks more professional. You can generate PayPal buttons if you have a PayPal business account.

If you are selling lesson packages (see Chapter 2), you can generate a dropdown menu, allowing users to select an appropriate package before clicking the 'Buy Now' button. Implementing PayPal and collecting payments will be discussed in more detail in Chapter 6.

Do the five-second test

Show your page to some friends or colleagues. Count to five, then close the page. Did they get the gist of your message? Was it clear what action needs to be taken? If not, keep tweaking.

It is important to note that you do not need to include all the previous elements on one page. If your template is restrictive, you can direct students to additional pages to view your scanned certificates, testimonials, payment area or contact form. However, it should be possible for students to book a lesson from any page on your site within one or two clicks. It is also imperative that you test your site on a mobile device; the path from browsing to booking a lesson should be simple and intuitive on a smartphone or small tablet, too.

Your terms and conditions page

A number of problems and misunderstandings can arise during an online course. These can include misunderstandings about the cancellation policy, misunderstandings about rescheduling lessons or confusion about when lesson packages expire. It is therefore a good idea to set out your terms and conditions on your website. This page can be accessed via the footer of your site, or it could be part of a FAQ (Frequently Asked Questions) page accessed from the header menu at the top.

For a sample set of terms and conditions see Chapter 5.

Your thank-you page

If you have implemented a payment button on your website (see Chapter 6), you should create a thank-you page that users will be taken to immediately after making a purchase. Your thank-you page should display the following information:

1. a message thanking the student for making a purchase

2. an instruction on how to schedule their first lesson (which might include a link to your online calendar).

You may also want to include a link to an online level-placement test, depending on how you have set up your workflow (see Chapter 5).

Creating posts

Having created your static business pages, you are ready to start posting. As explained earlier, most website-building tools distinguish posts from pages. Posts are usually created in your platform's dashboard. When published, they appear on a special page on your site, in the order that they are published. You can configure a Blogger or WordPress blog to display an excerpt of each post with a **Read More** button that takes readers to the full post. Blogging platforms typically allow you to include a 'feature image' in the post, which will be displayed with the text, and can also be included in the post excerpt.

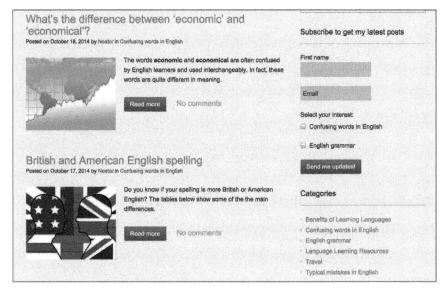

Post excerpts in a WordPress blog.

Make sure that you utilise the sidebar of your post template. Including an image, brief author bio and a link to your business page will help to convert casual visitors into paying students. The sidebar can also be used enhance your marketing strategies, for example by including an email sign-up form (see Chapter 4).

Conclusion

While building a blog involves an initial learning curve, there are considerable advantages. The ability to enrol students independently, create your own brand and the potential to reach a wide audience with your ideas are just a few of the benefits. Once successfully built, you will need to start driving traffic to your pages and boost engagement (commenting, social sharing, etc.). We will look at promotional strategies for your blog in the next chapter.

Further resources

WordPress vs. Weebly
http://www.websitebuilderexpert.com/weebly-vs-wordpress-whats-the-difference/

Blogger vs. WordPress vs. Weebly
http://www.techlila.com/blogger-vs-wordpress-com-vs-weebly/

WordPress vs. Blogger
http://www.makeuseof.com/tag/blogger-vs-wordpress-comparision/

http://www.shoutmeloud.com/wordpress-or-blogger-seo.html

Blogger resources
https://support.google.com/blogger/answer/42348?hl=en

https://support.google.com/blogger/answer/165955?hl=en

http://www.bloggertipspro.com/2012/06/creating-blogger-static-home-page.html

Self-hosted WordPress documentation and resources
http://codex.wordpress.org

Page builder for WordPress (allows you to design pages in a self-hosted WordPress site using an intuitive drag-and-drop editor)
http://www.wpbeaverbuilder.com

Chapter 4:

Promoting a blog

In Chapter 3, we looked at how to set up an English language teaching blog to attract prospective students. Once you have your website up and running, do not expect immediate results. You will need to work to promote your blog and start building traffic. Some of the tactics outlined in Chapter 2 (eg. commenting on forums and YouTube marketing) can be used for this purpose. However, there are other free and inexpensive strategies that are more specifically intended to increase your posts' exposure, encourage sharing and promote engagement. These include:

- search engine optimisation
- Facebook marketing
- exploiting other social networks
- email marketing.

This chapter will help you to get the most out of these various channels. In the final section, we will examine ways of monitoring your progress and optimising your marketing strategy.

Search engine optimisation (SEO)

Publishing posts on a regular basis will help your site get found in search engines such as Google, Bing and Yahoo!. This strategy has a gradual, cumulative effect, so you need to be patient and monitor your progress over time. Your initial efforts *will* pay off in the long run.

Google's ranking factors

It helps to have a basic knowledge of how search engines rank websites. Focus on Google in particular, as it is still the world's most popular search engine by far. When determining a webpage's rank in its search results pages,

Google takes into account over 200 signals, many of which you have little or no control over. For practical purposes, it is only really necessary to be familiar with a few on-site and off-site factors.

On-site factors

Search engines use 'robots' to 'crawl' the internet. When they come across a new webpage, the document is stored in Google's index database. This index is sorted alphabetically by search term, with each entry storing a list of documents in which the term appears and the location within the text where it occurs. A page will be considered more relevant for a given search query if the search term is found in key positions such as the main heading or page title. For example, a large heading 'English lessons via Skype' at the top of a webpage is a strong signal of relevancy for the query 'English lessons via Skype'. In recent years, Google has also become much more sophisticated in interpreting its users' intent. This means that the same page may be deemed relevant to closely related queries such as 'learn English online', 'I want to learn English on Skype', 'Skype English learning', 'looking for a Skype English teacher', etc.

It is important to remember that your ability to achieve a high-ranking position is relative to the competition. It is much easier to rank on the first page of Google's search results when there are relatively few other webpages competing for the same search term. But for a highly competitive English language query such as 'learn English online', do not expect to rank anywhere near Page 1.

However, getting your blog discovered in Google is not about ranking at the top for a popular search term. Every month, there are potentially millions of longer, more descriptive searches related to learning English. Each individual search query might only be entered into the Google search bar a few times, but it is the combined number of searches that matters. In the SEO industry, these less popular queries are known as 'long-tail keywords' (visualise a dinosaur whose long tail carries most of the creature's body weight). Examples of long-tail keywords might include 'what is the difference between see and hear', 'how can I pronounce the endings of past simple verbs', 'how to use say and tell' and 'how to achieve band 7.5 in the IELTS speaking test'.

In general, a less popular keyword means fewer competing webpages and a greater chance of ranking at the top. By publishing regular posts on a variety of 'less competitive' topics, you are helping your site rank for an increasing number of search terms. This will lead to a continuous overall growth in visitors.

Optimising posts for search engines

In order to maximise your long-tail strategy, make sure that your key phrases feature in strategic positions in your posts. Here are some places you should pay special attention to:

Page headings

Page headings are the headlines of your page, usually displayed above paragraphs of text. In HTML, page headings are denoted by the tags <h1>, <h2>, <h3>, etc. (for example, <h1>How to Master TOEFL Writing</h1>). With some website builders such as Weebly, you can create headings by dragging a 'Title' element onto your page. Despite the name of the element, this is technically a page heading, not a page title (as far as browser terminology is concerned). With other platforms such as WordPress, there is a special field (usually at the top of the post editor) that will generate the main heading.

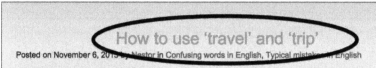

How to use 'travel' and 'trip'

Posted on November 6, 2015 by Nestor in Confusing words in English, Typical mistakes in English

Take a look at this sentence:

I had a very good travel.

This statement contains a very common mistake, even among more advanced learners. In natural English, we cannot use the word **travel** in this way. The noun **travel** is *uncountable* and it has a general meaning.

For example, we can say:

- **Travel** broadens the mind.
- I really like talking about **travel**.
- I'm browsing a website about **travel**

It is more often used as a 'modifier', for example:

- Paul is a **travel agent**.
- I found a special offer in this **travel brochure.**
- I like reading **travel blogs.**

eakeronline.com/typical-mistakes-in-english/how-to-use-travel-and-trip

Include important keywords or phrases in your page headings, but make sure they read naturally.

The page title

The page title is the text that shows up in the page tab at the top of your browser. It is also displayed in search results. In HTML, the page title is contained in the <title> tag, for example <title>How to use 'travel' and 'trip'</title>. All website builders and blogging platforms should allow you to easily edit your page titles. In some editors like Weebly, you will need to go into the advanced settings of the page.

A good title will include your keywords and website name or address, for example:

Useful tips for the FCE Speaking test – yourdomain.com

The page title often contains the same text as the main page heading by default. In WordPress you can manipulate the format of the title text with special SEO plugins (see the resources section at the end of this chapter). However, if your platform is using your main heading as the page title, this will normally be good enough.

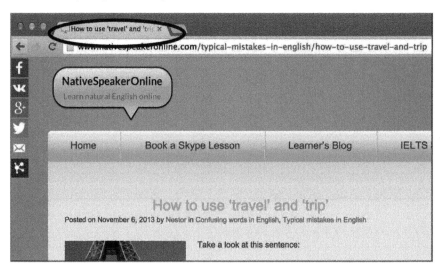

The page title of a post

The body of the page

Try to include relevant keywords throughout the page, but make sure the post reads naturally. It may be helpful to include synonyms of your target keywords in your post, for example 'Cambridge English First' as well as 'FCE'. Search engines are getting better at interpreting meaning, however, so there is no need to obsess too much over this.

Avoid 'keyword stuffing'

The practice of overpopulating a webpage with target keywords to influence its search engine rank is known as 'keyword stuffing'. Google's algorithm has long been able to detect this practice and will negatively rank websites that engage in this activity.

Optimising pages for search engines

Optimising your pages, for example your business pages or your home page, involves many of the same strategies as posts. However, there is one more area that you will want to pay attention to:

The page description

A page description (technically called a meta description) is a snippet of text that serves as a preview of a given page in search results. In HTML, it is contained in the tag <meta name="description">, for example <meta name="description" content="In this post, you will learn the differences between say and tell.">

The meta description is displayed only in search results pages – it does not appear in your actual pages or posts. If there is no meta description, Google will try to extract text for the preview description from elsewhere on your page. The text is pulled from wherever Google considers relevant to the search query. Meta descriptions can vary in length, but search engines will generally truncate (cut off) anything longer than around 160 characters.

Keywords in the meta description are not factored in to Google's ranking algorithm, so there is no need to optimise it for ranking. However, since the text is displayed in results pages, a compelling description will increase the likelihood of a user clicking on your result.

It is unnecessary to write meta descriptions for most of your posts. This is because in the absence of a meta description, Google is more likely to extract text that closely relates to the user's search query. Let's say an English learner searches for a particular idiom featured in one of your posts. Google may try to use text surrounding the idiom as the description of your page in its search results. In such cases, this description will be more relevant to the searcher's query than any fixed meta description you have written. Crafting a unique meta description for every single post is also tedious work, and the additional effort will outweigh any benefits.

Your pages are a different story, however. For your business pages, it will benefit you to craft compelling descriptions, as these pages are more commercial in nature. In addition, social sharing sites like Facebook commonly use the description tag when a page is shared on their site. You therefore want control over this text.

With some website builders such as Weebly, you will need to go into the advanced settings of a page to create or modify its description. In WordPress, you can add custom meta descriptions with a special SEO plugin (see the resources section at the end of this chapter).

Best practice for writing page descriptions:

- Try to create a sense of anticipation in order to encourage the user to click on your page.

- Grab the user's attention by communicating your message clearly and concisely without getting into fine details.

- Keep your meta descriptions between 150 and 160 characters in length.

- Include important keywords in the description: these won't help you rank highly but they will be highlighted in bold when they match the searcher's query.

- Try to include a call to action to elicit the response you want the user to take, eg. 'Book your free trial lesson today'.

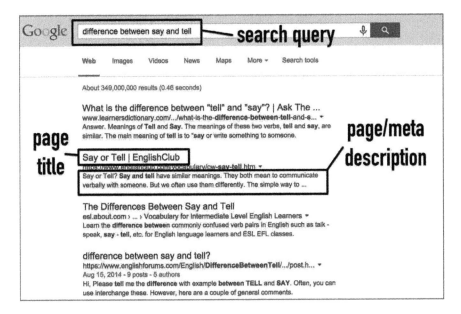

(Google and the Google logo are registered trademarks of Google Inc., used with permission.)

Off-site factors

Google's ranking algorithm attempts to determine the quality of a webpage as well as its relevance. As the search engine is not endowed with artificial intelligence and therefore cannot make judgments about a website the way a human would, Google looks for scalable on-site and off-site quality signals. One of the most important off-site signals is the number of links pointing at a webpage from other websites. These links are called 'backlinks'. The idea, patented by Google, is based on the principle that linking to another website is generally considered to be an endorsement of that site (think of links as votes). Google was the first search engine to introduce backlinks as a key ranking factor, which resulted in vastly improved results and allowed them to attract lots of users and dominate the search market.

Predictably, SEO professionals and spammers quickly found ways to manipulate the system by implementing artificial large scale link-building techniques. Google responded by refining their algorithm and developed ways of detecting whether a link is 'genuine' or acquired by spam tactics. Nowadays, not all backlinks are considered equal – some do not count at all and others may even have a negative impact on a site's ranking if they are found to violate Google's guidelines.

Acquiring links

There are two typical ways of acquiring links:

- link building
- link earning.

As the term implies, link building involves a manual process. This activity includes posting links in forums, submitting links to directories, commenting on blogs and persuading or paying webmasters (people who run websites) to link to your site. Be aware that buying links is against Google's guidelines and may have a negative effect on your site's ranking if detected by their algorithms. If you engage in any form of link building, make sure you are getting links from credible websites relevant to language learning or teaching. At the end of this chapter, you can find further resources on link-building strategies if you are interested. Despite their importance as a ranking factor, it is not necessary to be familiar with all the intricacies of building links. Just keep in mind the following general rule of thumb: the easier a link is to acquire, the less valuable it is from a ranking perspective. For example, putting a link to your website in a forum post signature (see Chapter 2) is unlikely to have a significant impact on your ranking, although it may lead to other benefits like referring forum members and visitors to your blog.

Link building can be time consuming and challenging. If you are new to internet marketing, the safest and most sustainable approach is link earning, that is, providing useful and engaging content that would make users want to link to you naturally. This approach allows you to focus exclusively on your content and it is increasingly recommended by marketing professionals.

You can monitor the backlinks that you are acquiring with a tracking tool such as Google Webmaster Tools (see page 80).

Final thoughts

As blogging tools and website builders develop and get more intuitive, it becomes easier for teachers to start their own blogs. Over time, this will lead to a greater number of webpages competing for search queries related to learning English. As a result, it may become increasingly challenging to rank on the first page of

Google for many long-tail keywords. The needs of English learners are vast, however, and it might be wise to focus on niches, or target a specific geographic region, rather than write about general English problems for a general audience.

Another trend to be aware of is personalised search. Google does not serve exactly the same results to every user. The search engine uses your browsing history and location to customise the results that you see, especially if you are logged in to Google. This means that the ranking positions of your posts may vary for each user. If someone is a frequent visitor to your blog and searches for a topic closely related to the theme of one of your posts, it is likely that your post will appear on the first page of Google. The same query performed by a user who has never visited your website may not trigger your post to be displayed on the first page.

Facebook marketing

With over one billion active users, Facebook is by far the most popular social networking site in the world. Exploiting Facebook to boost your website traffic can be achieved by encouraging social sharing and creating a Facebook page for your blog. Be aware that Facebook often changes its interface and any of the specific steps and recommendations mentioned in this section may become outdated.

Enable sharing

Enable readers to share your content by adding Facebook 'share' buttons to your posts. This should be relatively easy to configure, depending on your blogging platform. One effective implementation option is to add a vertical social sharing bar that floats on the left of the page and follows users as they scroll (but at the same time doesn't annoy them by obscuring any of your content). The share bar can be configured to include other social networks where you think your users might be active. Links to tools and plugins are included in the resources section at the end of this chapter.

Create a Facebook page

Consider creating a Facebook page for your blog. To create a page, go to www.facebook.com/pages/create and select a category such as Brand or Product > Website (you will be able to choose a more precise category later when you edit your About section). Follow the on-screen instructions to complete your page.

A well-performing Facebook page will help increase your exposure and web traffic. When it comes to design, study the following recommendations.

Cover image
When Facebook users land on your page, you want them to figure out who you are and what you do within a few seconds. This is why a good cover image is important. Marketing professionals recommend a number of best practices and strategies for designing covers. As an online tutor, the following suggestions might help boost the performance of your page:

- Use an image that relates to you or your tuition service. Don't use an image of something unrelated and random such as a cat, for example.

- Use an image that is at least 851 x 315 pixels. Facebook will expand any image that is smaller than these dimensions, which will make your cover look blurred.

- Include a 'call-to-action' message in your image, for example 'Book a Lesson Today' and include a link to your business page in the image description.

- Change the image from time to time to reflect seasons and festive periods.

In the resources section at the end of this chapter, there are several free and inexpensive image editing tools that you can use to modify images and overlay text.

Profile photo

Users who land on your Facebook page will get their first impressions from your cover photo. However, it is your profile picture that they will see most often. Your profile picture appears in:

- the News Feeds of your fans (people who have 'liked' your page)
- posts on your page's timeline
- comments that you make on your page
- comments that you make on other pages while using your page
- your website's Facebook Like box (see below).

It is best to upload a square image as rectangular images must be cropped as square. The profile photo that you upload must be at least 180 x 180 pixels, but it will be displayed at 160 x 160 pixels and resized to smaller dimensions in the News Feed and when displayed next to your posts.

Complete your About section

An incomplete About section could result in missed traffic to your website. Since Facebook shows a short description of your page under the profile picture on your timeline, you will want to craft a compelling message and include a link to your website.

To edit the short description for your page, click the pencil icon in the About box. Try to follow these tips suggested by marketers:

- Type in your URL at the beginning of your description, so that it's the first thing people see.
- Be concise and clear.
- Use up to 100 characters (155 is the maximum).
- Don't resort to keyword stuffing.

You can also edit the category of your page in your About section. At this stage, you will be able to choose a more suitable category than earlier in the sign up process. Here you can select **Website & Blogs > Education Website**.

Make your website 'like'-able

Encourage users to 'like' your page by adding a Facebook icon or widget to your blog. Most themes and templates come with social media buttons in the header, sidebar or footer, which you can easily configure to link to your social media pages. If you have a WordPress blog, you can add a Facebook Like box widget to the sidebar of your posts which can display the following:

- a link to your Facebook page

- a Like button allowing users to like your website on Facebook without the need to visit your Facebook page

- a stream of your latest Facebook posts

- sample profile photos of people who liked your page.

If you don't have a WordPress blog, you can generate the code to display the Like box from Facebook's developers website and then paste it in an embed code widget or element. See the resources section at the end of this chapter for further details.

Share content on Facebook

Having created your Facebook page, you can now share new blog posts and other creative content with your fans. If your content is engaging, they will 'like' or share it, enabling you to grow your fan base organically. Unfortunately, Facebook has recently been restricting the exposure that pages get in News Feeds, giving prominence to the most engaging posts. Facebook claim this is due to the increase in content competing for limited News Feed space. Some marketing commentators, on the other hand, argue that this is a ploy designed to force members to use Facebook's advertising platform (see Chapter 2) to reach their own fans. Whatever the case, it is clear that your posts need to be as engaging as possible. Here are a few recommendations:

- Try to keep your posts between 100 and 250 characters. Shorter, succinct posts are better received.

- Share your blog posts when you publish them and make sure they have featured images, which will be displayed in your Facebook timeline and in the News Feed.

- Post images to get more attention. If you include a hyperlink in the text part of your post, use a URL shortening service such as goo.gl to make the link look neater.

- Ask your fans to comment on images or videos.

- Share a promotion from time to time, eg. 25% off course prices for this month.

- Try to relate some of your posts to current events or holidays.

- Try to keep to a regular posting schedule.

Final thoughts

A running theme in the marketing sections of this book has been credibility, a key ingredient for attracting students and enabling you to charge a higher price than the market average. The social proof of a popular Facebook page is a particularly reliable indicator of credibility. However, building a large fan base takes time, so consider using Facebook's advertising platform (see Chapter 2) to give yourself a head start. By promoting a well-performing post to a targeted audience, you can acquire a lot of new fans at relatively low cost.

Other social networks

If you intend to promote your blog on social media, Facebook should be the only social network you need due to its extensive user base. However, experimenting with other networks might bring you improved results, depending on the needs and geographic location of your target students and visitors. Here are three alternative social media platforms you might consider:

Twitter (Twitter.com)

Twitter is a social networking tool for posting very short updates, comments or thoughts. These are called tweets. Using Twitter can help drive traffic to your blog and attract attention to your tuition service. As of 2014, Twitter had over 500 million users, more than 271 million of whom are active users.[1] It can be assumed that this figure includes a significant number of English language learners.

---

1 https://investor.twitterinc.com/releasedetail.cfm?ReleaseID=862505

Your Twitter profile

If you don't already have a Twitter profile, visit Twitter.com and sign up. You will notice five key elements that make up your profile:

- your Twitter handle (username)
- your name
- a description
- a link to your website
- your profile and header images.

Your Twitter handle should be the same as, or related to, the name of your blog. Be aware that Twitter limits the length of tweets to 140 characters. If the name of your blog is rather long, try to condense it to make it easier for someone to mention you in their messages. For example, consider @mikeenglish if the name of your blog is 'Mike's English Studio'.

For your profile name, you will want to use your real name or a descriptive name that includes your name, eg. 'Teacher Tim'. People find it easier to identify with a person rather than a brand.

Twitter allows you to include a profile and header image, which essentially serve the same purpose as a Facebook page profile and cover image. The current recommendations are 400 x 400 pixels for profile images and 1500 x 500 pixels for header images. Like all social networks, current specifications do not preclude future changes and you should try to keep up-to-date with any future redesigns that Twitter decides to roll out.

Building your following

To be successful on Twitter, you will need to amass a large following. This will take some time and effort, but it is far from unreachable. Follow these recommendations:

- Ensure that your Twitter profile information is complete.
- Make a habit of tweeting as often as possible. The more you post on Twitter, the more likely people will notice you and decide to follow you. You can take advantage of the message length limitation and tweet 'on the go'.
- Promote your Twitter account by placing links on your website, social networking profiles and teacher marketplace profiles if applicable. You can also include your Twitter account in email signatures.

- Try to find prospective students to follow using Twitter's search engine. People who you follow will often follow you back if your profile resonates with their interests. You can find these Twitter users by using the search facility to search for tweets and profiles that include relevant keywords such as 'learning English'.

- Follow people who follow you. This is considered good practice because people who notice that you haven't followed them back might unfollow you.

Tips for tweeting

The advantage of Twitter's 140 character limit is that you can serve your followers with regular bite-sized lessons. Here are some tips for tweeting:

- Shorten URL links in your tweets using a service such as tinyurl.com or goo.gl.

- Make use of the hashtag (#) to label the topic of the tweet and increase the chances of your post being discovered by other users.

- Use the @ symbol before someone's Twitter username to have a direct, albeit still public, conversation.

- Occasionally ask your followers to retweet something. (According to marketing professionals, this does work!)

- Pin selected tweets to the top of your profile page.

- Tweet images as well as text. (Image tweets get 18% more clicks and 150% more retweets than those without.)

- Consider repeating your most popular tweets a few times. (Make sure the posts are around 8–12 hours apart.) This will help you reach the people who missed your updates the first time around.

When it comes to content, you can tweet just about anything you think might be useful for your followers. Here are some ideas:

- Link to a post on your blog.

- Link to useful video or other resource.

- Announce a special promotion.

- Tweet an idiom of the day.

- Tweet a phrasal verb of the day.

- Tweet an exam tip of the day.

LinkedIn (linkedin.com)

With over 250 million users, LinkedIn is a popular social networking service for business people. It might be a great place to network and market yourself as a business English tutor. To make the most of LinkedIn, include a link to your blog in your profile and contribute to discussions related to business English.

You might have success by joining a group for non-native English speaking professionals who need to use English in their work. However, make sure your interests are somehow aligned with those of the group and that you are able contribute constructively to discussions. (It helps if you have some actual business experience or expertise.) Posting in a way that blatantly promotes yourself will likely lead to immediate banning. Read the group profile carefully before joining.

Vkontakte (Vk.com)

VK (Originally VKontakte, Russian: вконтакте) is a social networking service available in several languages but particularly popular among Russian-speaking users around the world, especially in Russia, Ukraine, Kazakhstan, Moldova, Belarus and Israel. As of November 2014, the network had over 280 million accounts.

VK allows you to create a personal profile and a community page for your blog, which is the network's equivalent of a Facebook page. Like boxes and share buttons can also be implemented on your website.

If your target market is the Russian speaking world, you may be interested to know that most Russian internet users spend about seven hours per day in VKontakte compared with 1.5 hours on Facebook, according to a 2014 research study. Be aware, however, that Russian Facebook users were found to have a higher level of income than their VK counterparts, according to the same survey.

Email marketing

Recent studies have shown that email is a more effective marketing channel than social media when it comes to selling. Building a list of opt-in email subscribers and sending automatic updates of new posts helps drive traffic to your blog, boost engagement and, most importantly, keeps your prospective students thinking about you. You should continually endeavour to convert your visitors, followers, potential students and even paying clients into subscribers.

Building your list

An email opt-in box in the sidebar of your blog can be used to capture a visitor's email address. Alternatively, you may want to experiment with a pop-up plugin configured to display your sign-up form after the visitor has spent a specified amount of time on your site. If you have a self-hosted blog, it is convenient to use an email marketing plugin such as MailPoet for WordPress and a low-cost third-party email delivery service such as Elastic Email (see the resources section at the end of this chapter). You can even encourage subscriptions via your Facebook page and YouTube channel, if you have one.

Composing and sending newsletters

You can configure your email plugin to send out emails to subscribers whenever a new post is published. Most email plugins let you create your own email templates including special tags within the email body for generating variables such as the subscriber's first name. The plugins should also provide an analytics tool that displays engagement and delivery statistics, such as the number of subscribers who read your email or who clicked a link to one of your posts.

Some email marketing tips:

- Don't include too many images in your emails.
- Use a readable font, eg. Arial 14pt.
- Use a larger font for the links in your emails to make them stand out.
- Personalise the emails: collect the user's first name via the sign-up form and include it in the opening salutation (eg. Hey <first name>).
- Experiment with frequency and timing.

Your email subscriber list is one of your most valuable assets. Whenever you have a special promotion, you can easily compose an email bulletin and send it to the entire list or a specified subset of that list.

Monitoring your progress

Online tracking tools help you measure the effectiveness of all your marketing efforts and better manage your valuable time. Google provides two valuable free tools: Google Analytics and Google Webmaster Tools. You can access both through your Google account.

Google Analytics

Google Analytics provides you with a wide range of useful data including how many people are visiting your website, which channels they are coming from, where in the world they are located, how much time they are spending on your site, which devices they are using and which pages they are visiting. This will help you make key decisions like scaling back on less effective areas and focusing on the strategies that are generating the best results.

For example, you may be spending the same amount of time on Twitter and Facebook, but it is possible that one of the two is generating significantly more traffic. Knowing this, you can decide to dedicate more of your time to Facebook, or even consider whether it is worth continuing with Twitter.

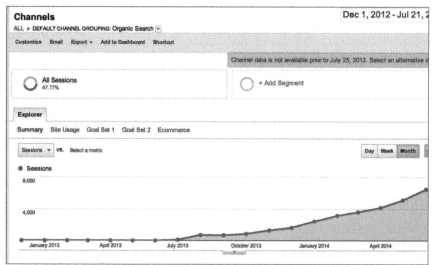

A Google Analytics graph showing traffic resulting from online search. (Google and the Google logo are registered trademarks of Google Inc., used with permission.)

To be able to use Google Analytics, you need to sign into Google Analytics (www.google.com/analytics/) with your regular Google account and then sign up for an Analytics account. Give the account a name, enter your website's URL, accept the terms and conditions and click the Create Account button. The platform will then generate a tracking ID and a script that you need to add your website. Some blog themes and platforms have special sections for the Google Analytics code. With a self-hosted WordPress blog, you can also install a Google Analytics plugin which facilitates the process (see the resources section at the end of this chapter). Once you have added the code to your site, there will be a delay before you start seeing data.

Google Webmaster Tools (optional)

Google Webmaster Tools provides you with detailed reports about your pages' visibility in Google, including which search queries are generating the most clicks, your average position for different search terms and which websites are linking to you. It provides a lot of other technical data about your site which you normally won't need to be concerned with. To sign up for Webmaster Tools, simply go to www.google.com/webmasters/tools, sign in with your Google account, click Add a Site, enter your site's URL and verify ownership via your Google Analytics account by checking the option 'Google Analytics'. As with Google Analytics, it may take a while for data to start appearing, even up to several days.

Conclusion

Building a successful blog takes some time and effort. The most time-consuming tasks include writing blog posts and editing photos. If you find this discouraging, be aware that you can eventually scale back on your content creation and marketing activities once you are generating the traffic you need to fill your online teaching schedule.

It is also important to remember that the promotional strategies covered in this chapter are options. If email marketing and Facebook are working well for you, there is little need to devote your precious free time to other channels. Monitoring your progress with Google Analytics will give you a clear picture of the effectiveness of all your marketing efforts.

Further reading and resources

Search engine optimisation

Moz: www.moz.com/learn/seo
These resources include free tips and guides on SEO, social media and link building.

Facebook marketing

Mari Smith: www.marismith.com
This website is run by one of the top Facebook marketing thought leaders and includes lots of free Facebook marketing advice.

Facebook Like button: https://developers.facebook.com/docs/plugins/like-button
Display a Facebook Like button on your website, enabling visitors to see how many users already like your page and allowing them to 'like' the page with one click, without needing to visit the page itself.

AddtoAny: www.addtoany.com/buttons
This website allows you to add and customise social-sharing buttons to your website.

Image editing tools

Gimp: www.gimp.org
Gimp is a free image editor that has many similar features to Adobe Photoshop and is available for Windows, Mac and Linux operating systems.

Pixelmator: www.pixelmator.com
Pixelmator is a powerful and user-friendly image editor available for Mac OS. The software costs only $29.99 and is free to try for 30 days.

Free WordPress plugins

WordPress SEO by Yoast: www.yoast.com/wordpress/plugins/seo
This plugin allows you to optimise your WordPress site for SEO.

MailPoet: www.mailpoet.com
This plugin allows you to build an email subscriber list as well as send newsletters and email notifications.

Email marketing

Elastic Email: www.elasticemail.com
Elastic Email is a simple, fast email delivery service for marketing email. Prices currently range from around $0.09-$0.99 / 1000 emails.

MailChimp: www.mailchimp.com
MailChimp offers a complete email marketing solution for small businesses. If your blogging platform does not currently support email marketing widgets such as MailPoet for WordPress, a service like MailChimp will allow you to generate code for subscription forms.

Google Analytics tutorials

Google Analytics:
https://marketingplatform.google.com/intl/en_uk/about/analytics/
These articles and videos provided by Google will help you become familiar with Google Analytics.

Chapter 5:

Establishing a workflow

When you are teaching online, an efficient workflow will help you organise your time better, convey professionalism and convert more potential students into paying clients. Since students' needs differ, it helps to develop a flexible approach. This chapter will cover the different elements of this flexible workflow:

- initial correspondence
- free consultations
- level placement testing
- trial lessons
- needs analysis
- establishing terms and conditions
- requesting and confirming payment
- devising a syllabus
- scheduling lessons.

If you are acquiring most of your students via a teacher marketplace (see Chapter 2), be aware that most marketplace platforms have their own workflow that members are required to follow.

Responding to initial enquiries

When students contact you to enquire about your courses, the same type of questions will appear again and again. It saves time to have some ready prepared email templates that you can simply copy and paste in your responses. Within the templates you can include links for appointment scheduling (see Chapter 1), online payment (see Chapter 6), etc. Here are some examples:

Hi <student name>

Thank you for your interest in taking lessons with me. I offer a free 20-minute trial consultation on Skype. During the consultation, we will discuss your needs and talk about how we can work together to reach your goals. To arrange an appointment, just click the link below:

<link to appointment scheduling tool>

I look forward to speaking to you.

Hi <student name>

Thank you for your email. I will be happy to talk about the lessons I offer. To schedule a free 20-minute consultation on Skype, just let me know three times and days when you are available. Here's my schedule:

<public link to Google Calendar>

Speak to you soon!

Hi <student name>

Thank you for your email. I will be happy to offer you a 30-minute trial lesson for $1. Please tell me something about yourself and your needs.

What kind of course are you interested in? What is your approximate level?

Speak to you soon!

Hi <student name>

Thank you for your email. I will be happy to offer you a trial lesson for $1. I first need to know something about you. Please click the link below and fill in the short form. It should take you less than five minutes.

<needs analysis form link>

Once you have submitted the form, please make a payment by clicking the link below:

<payment link>

Speak to you soon!

Free consultation

Consider offering a free consultation for prospective students on your website or in your advertising. The session should be fairly short (eg. 20 minutes) and can serve a number of different purposes. In particular, the consultation is an opportunity to:

- introduce yourself and build some early rapport
- check the quality of the internet connection between you and the prospective student
- discover the prospective student's needs
- ascertain his or her approximate level
- promote yourself and your tuition service
- arrange or discuss a future lesson schedule
- have the prospective student subscribe to your blog if you have one.

You can experiment a little with the structure of the consultation, as long as you try to cover the basic elements outlined above.

Although you are not delivering a formal lesson per se, you can still apply reformulation techniques (see Chapter 7) while your prospective student is talking. Consider including your corrections in a Google sheet (see Chapter 1) and sharing them as a sample of your approach as well as something tangible to take away from the session. This will increase your chances of converting the prospective student into a paying client.

Here are some additional tips to help you conduct a successful consultation:

- Always display a photo of yourself in your Skype profile.

- Use video if the connection is good enough (the student will trust you more if you show your face), but don't insist on the student using video and be aware of cultural sensitivities.

- Try not to interrupt the student too much while he or she is talking.

- Encourage the student to ask you questions as well.

- Take notes using your favourite note-taking tool (eg. Google Docs, Evernote, Microsoft Word) or record the session with a Skype recording tool (see Chapter 1).

- Be prepared to answer questions about your terms and conditions (your cancellation policy, lesson package validity periods, etc.)

- Try to get the student to commit to a lesson package deal at the end of the session, but don't pressurise him or her.

- Smile, stay relaxed and make the session pleasant: try not to come across as too stiff or 'over-professional'.

Checking the connection and troubleshooting call-quality issues

If both you and the student are using broadband internet, you should generally be able to hear and see each other without too many problems. However, there may be a lag in communication, which can create situations where teacher and student find themselves talking over each other or hear their own voices echoed back to them. To solve this issue, always give students a few seconds to think over the answer to a question and insist on their wearing a headset if you can hear your own voice emitted from the student's speakers.

Poor call quality might result from a hardware misconfiguration, application settings or a slow internet connection. As the provider of the tuition service, you will be expected to troubleshoot any problems, so make sure you are familiar with the typical solutions for solving common call-quality issues. Skype provides articles detailing troubleshooting solutions on their website. Visit www.skype.com, click **Help** and search for 'solving quality problems'.

If hardware or settings are not responsible for the problem, it is likely that the student has a slow internet connection. Symptoms of a poor connection issue include frequently dropped calls, pixelated video, robotic sounds or words being cut off. To diagnose a connection issue, check whether the student has the minimum bandwidth required to make the voice or video call (see Chapter 1). This can be done by having the student perform an online speed test using a tool such as www.speedtest.net. If the results turn out to be well below Skype's recommendations, inform the student that online tuition will unfortunately not be possible unless he or she can access a better connection.

In cases where there may be adequate bandwidth, the following suggestions might help improve the quality:

- if you are using video, turn it off
- close any other open windows and applications that are using the internet
- if connected via Wi-Fi, ensure that there is a strong wireless signal: move closer to the router if necessary
- restart Skype.

As broadband internet technology continues to develop, VoIP call quality should become less of an issue. However, it is better to discover any serious technical hindrances before the student has paid for any tuition.

Level placement

There are different approaches to determining a student's level, depending on the type of student and tuition service that you are offering. Any of the following evaluation methods are possible.

- Make an informal judgement based on initial correspondence.
- Ask if the student has studied English before and what level was attained.

- Conduct a 15-minute oral test. (See the resources section at the end of this chapter for a sample speaking level guide.)

- Have the student complete an online test form.

- Try a combination of these methods.

Test forms consisting of multiple-choice questions can be created using Google Forms and shared with students via a link (see Chapter 1). In the resources section at the end of this chapter, there are links to sample level placement tests that you can use or adapt.

Needs analysis

Discovering a student's needs and expectations will help you provide a customised course and select appropriate resources (see Chapter 7). This will result in a satisfied and loyal client.

Conducting a needs analysis can be a formal or informal procedure. Needs can be discovered casually by asking open questions during an initial session or gleaned from the initial email correspondence. The analysis can be complicated by the fact that many students expect the teacher to decide the course content and will not have a clear idea of what they want to do, hence the need for a flexible approach.

The following scenarios are typical examples of students' needs:

- The student travels a lot and needs to communicate better.

- The student is preparing for a job interview in English.

- The student needs to achieve Band 7 in the IELTS Speaking test in order to study abroad.

- The student needs to use English at work – telephoning, presentations, writing emails, using industry-specific vocabulary, etc.

- The student needs English for work and travel.

While many teachers prefer an informal approach, a detailed needs analysis form might be suitable for business English students, who tend to have a clearer idea of what they want to learn and who may expect to be provided with a structured course syllabus. Even with elementary business English students, whose language needs will normally encompass core language elements, there may be very specific additional needs. You can find examples of needs analysis forms in the resources section at the end of this chapter.

The most efficient way to collect the data is to design an online form using a form building tool such as Google Forms (see Chapter 1). You can design multiple needs analysis forms catering for different niches or stages in your workflow. Here are some examples:

- a short form for collecting basic information to help you conduct a trial lesson

- a more detailed form to help you prepare a tailored business English syllabus after the student has purchased a lesson package

- a form for collecting information on the student's perceived strengths and weaknesses (eg. for an exam preparation course).

Proposing a course plan based on an informal needs analysis

Having established the student's general needs, talk about what you can offer to meet those needs. Below are some examples:

- 'We will spend 50% of the lesson on conversation and 50% doing grammar work from PDF worksheets.'

- 'We will do lots of job interview role plays and learn key vocabulary using PDF and online resources.'

- 'We will practise sample questions for each part of the TOEFL speaking section and I will provide you with feedback on your performance and some tips on how to improve.'

- 'We will follow a structured syllabus tailored to your needs: lessons will be based on PDF resources, dialogues and video.'

Make sure your proposal is aligned with the student's expectations. A student who has a clear idea of what he or she wants to do may prefer to decide on the course plan or lesson format. This could sometimes lead to conflicts between needs and wants. For example, the student may need to improve his or her grammar, but may want to focus exclusively on speaking practice.

Such situations can pose a dilemma. If you try to enforce your own ideas, you risk discouraging a potential client. However, if you feel very strongly that a particular kind of course is needed, you may be able to persuade the student to accept your proposal. The best approach will probably be a compromise with the balance in favour of the student's suggestion.

Trial lesson

If you want to encourage more students to enrol, consider offering a short (eg. 30-minute) trial lesson. Many teachers provide the session at no charge. However, there are several good reasons to avoid offering free lessons:

- You may attract students who are not serious about improving their English and have no intention of making a purchase.
- You will invite students who are not capable of making online payments.
- Some students may interpret the offer to mean free lessons for life.
- Google may start ranking you for keywords such as 'free online English tutor', which will attract the wrong kind of student.

In order to discourage time wasters and avoid a great deal of frustration, successful online teachers have found that the best solution is to offer the trial lesson for a negligible sum, eg. $1 for 20 minutes. This allows you to attract students who are serious about learning and understand what is involved. At the same time, you filter out students who are unable to make online payments, eg. students whose countries are not supported by PayPal. When you gain more experience and have very few available time slots left, you might decide not to offer any discount on your trial lesson in order to discourage all but the most serious prospective students.

You should have some suitable activities or lesson plans ready to use in the trial session (see Chapter 7). The table below presents a few ideas.

Table 5.1: First lesson ideas

General need	Ideas for first lesson
Speaking practice	Use a speaking level guide (see resources at the end of this chapter). Let the student talk about his or her interests. Provide correction.
Grammar	Present simple vs. present continuous (worksheet)
Business English	Introductions (worksheet, dialogue) Talking about job and company
Exam preparation (IELTS, TOEFL, etc.)	Mock speaking test with feedback

If you are teaching in a marketplace (see Chapter 2), bear in mind that students are going to be trying out lots of different teachers, so you might want to experiment with a slightly unconventional lesson plan in order to stand out. Teacher marketplace rules tend to limit the number of trial lessons that members are allowed to take in order to prevent students from exploiting the platform for free tuition.

Follow-up

If the student did not commit to a lesson package at the end of the free consultation or trial lesson, consider applying some polite, gentle pressure. Send an email thanking the student for taking the session with you, summarise what you have talked about and remind him or her to subscribe to your blog if you have one. Publishing blog posts is a very effective way to keep the student thinking about you without coming across as pushy or needy (which is likely to give the impression that you don't have many students).

If the student has not contacted you after a few days, you can follow up. Ask if he or she has come to a decision or whether there is anything else you can do to help. If you feel that the student was not serious in the first place, was discouraged by your prices, or if for some reason the lesson didn't go well, forget about it and move on. With time, you will be able to gauge levels of interest more effectively and become more selective about who you decide to chase up.

Requesting and confirming payment

If the student decides to purchase a lesson package, send a thank-you email. Provide or confirm your payment details by attaching an electronic bill, sending a PayPal payment request or including instructions on how to pay via your website. If you have enabled payments on your site, students will often simply make the purchase before communicating their decision, and you will receive an automatic email notification from PayPal as soon as the payment has been processed. The next chapter will look at billing methods and online payment implementation.

If applicable, include a link to your business English needs analysis form and ask the student to submit it before the first lesson so that you can prepare a tailored syllabus. It is also a good idea to include a link to your terms and conditions page, if you have one.

Scheduling lessons

Lessons can be scheduled manually or using an appointment booking tool that enables the student to reserve a slot in your online calendar (see Chapter 1). If you are scheduling lessons manually, follow these recommendations:

- adopt a convention, for example, always use the student's time zone

- when you make an appointment, confirm the time in the Skype chat or by email so that the student has a written record of it. Quote the time zone, eg. 10pm Saudi time

- record your lessons in a calendar tool such as Google Calendar.

Devising a structured syllabus based on a needs analysis form

Some students who have bought a lesson package may expect to be provided with a tailored syllabus. In such cases, a completed online needs analysis form will provide the information needed to devise a structured course plan incorporating the four skills (reading, writing, listening and speaking), phonology, grammar, and periodic revision. The course content can be based on your own materials or resources and ideas such as those presented in Chapter 7. If applicable, you can incorporate the European framework grammar requirements in the grammar part of the syllabus (see the resources section at the end of this chapter).

An evolving tailored syllabus can be prepared using a Google Sheet (see Chapter 1) and shared with the student before the first lesson. The student can review the plan and be encouraged to propose changes. During the course, new needs may arise and these can be incorporated into the Google Sheet syllabus.

Case study

Alessandro is a 40-year-old Italian manager at upper-intermediate (B2) level. He needs English in order to communicate better with his native English business associates, especially on the phone and via email. He would also like to become more confident at giving opinions during meetings. He enjoys travelling and often works remotely, usually from cafés. He would like to incorporate fluency practice into every lesson and receive reading materials before each lesson.

Alessandro's course consists of two lessons per week. Here's what his Google Sheet syllabus might look like for the first month.

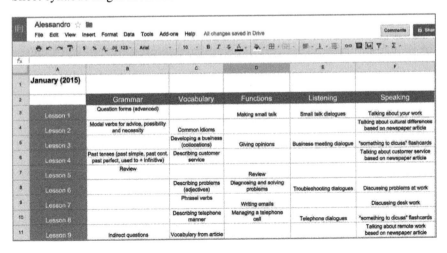

	Grammar	Vocabulary	Functions	Listening	Speaking
January (2015)					
Lesson 1	Question forms (advanced)		Making small talk	Small talk dialogues	Talking about your work
Lesson 2	Modal verbs for advice, possibility and necessity	Common idioms			Talking about cultural differences based on newspaper article
Lesson 3		Developing a business (collocations)	Giving opinions	Business meeting dialogue	"something to dicuss" flashcards
Lesson 4	Past tenses (past simple, past cont. past perfect, used to + infinitive)	Describing customer service			Talking about customer service based on newspaper article
Lesson 5	Review		Review		
Lesson 6		Describing problems (adjectives)	Diagnosing and solving problems	Troubleshooting dialogues	Discussing problems at work
Lesson 7		Phrasal verbs	Writing emails		Discussing desk work
Lesson 8		Describing telephone manner	Managing a telephone call	Telephone dialogues	"something to dicuss" flashcards
Lesson 9	Indirect questions	Vocabulary from article			Talking about remote work based on newspaper article

(Google and the Google logo are registered trademarks of Google Inc., used with permission.)

Terms and conditions

If you have a website, you should have a terms and conditions page (see Chapter 3). Alternatively, you can prepare an online document using Google Docs. It is important to communicate your terms early on in your workflow, for example by linking to them in your email correspondence.

Terms and conditions help avoid disruptions to your teaching schedule, misunderstandings and lost revenue as a result of technical problems, late cancellations, no shows and late appearances on Skype.

Here's a sample set of terms and conditions:

1. Your lesson credits can be used within 60 days from the date of receipt of your payment. You will lose any credits that you did not use within 60 days.

2. You can change the time or day of a scheduled lesson at least four hours before the start of the lesson.

3. If you miss a lesson without cancelling before the agreed upon deadline, you will lose the credit for that lesson.

4. If you are late for a scheduled lesson, you will lose the credit for the minutes you missed. For example, if a lesson starts at 5pm and you appear on Skype at 5.20pm, the duration of the lesson will be 40 minutes.

5. Make sure you have the required minimum download/upload connection speed of 500kbps (test your connection speed with www.speedtest.net).

6. If the call quality is too poor to conduct a lesson after 20 minutes of trying to establish a good connection, the lesson will be cancelled and rescheduled for free at a convenient future date.

Conclusion

This chapter has covered the main components of an online teaching workflow, from responding to initial enquiries to scheduling the first official lessons. As you can see in the examples below, the complexity of the workflow will depend on the niche that you are targeting and the type of enquiries that you receive.

If you are providing business English tuition and your potential client requires a syllabus as well as invoices for services rendered, your workflow may look like this:

Workflow 1 (consultation)

Respond to initial enquiry ➜ Free consultation (15 minutes) ➜ Follow up ➜ Email bill for lesson package ➜ Schedule first lesson ➜ Full needs analysis and level placement test ➜ Syllabus preparation ➜ Syllabus presentation ➜ First official lesson

Workflow 2 (trial lesson)

Respond to initial enquiry ➜ Short needs analysis ➜ Trial lesson for $1 (30 minutes) ➜ Follow up ➜ Email bill for lesson package ➜ Schedule first lesson ➜ Full needs analysis ➜ Syllabus preparation ➜ Syllabus presentation ➜ First official lesson

Workflow 3 (consultation + trial lesson)

Respond to initial enquiry ➜ Free consultation (15 minutes) ➜ Trial lesson for $1 (30 minutes) ➜ Follow up ➜ Email bill for lesson package ➜ Schedule first lesson ➜ Full needs analysis ➜ Syllabus preparation ➜ Syllabus presentation ➜ First official lesson

If a prospective student is interested in simple conversation lessons and eventually purchases a lesson package on your website, your workflow might look something like this:

Workflow 1 (trial lesson)

Respond to initial enquiry ➜ Trial lesson for $1 (30 minutes) ➜ Follow up ➜ Confirm online payment ➜ Schedule first lesson ➜ First official lesson

> ## Workflow 2 (consultation without initial enquiry)
>
> Free consultation ➔ Confirm online payment ➔ Schedule first lesson ➔ First official lesson

Further reading and resources

Needs analysis articles, worksheets and forms

OnestopEnglish: http://www.onestopenglish.com/business/teaching-approaches/needs-analysis/

Level placement tests

The British Council provides a free online level test, with the result being one of three possible levels:

- beginner to pre-intermediate
- intermediate
- upper intermediate or above.

https://learnenglish.britishcouncil.org/online-english-level-test

Cambridge English also has free online tests, for different ages and language preferences, for example, General English, Business English and Young Learners, to identify which Cambridge exam might be advisable (another way to identify level).

https://www.cambridgeenglish.org/test-your-english/

Grammar to study at each CEFR (Common European Framework of Reference for Languages) level

Exam English: http://www.examenglish.com/CEFR/cefr_grammar.htm

Chapter 6:

Getting paid

Once you have decided on a pricing strategy for your service (see Chapter 2), you will need to enable students to pay you online. This is crucial to the success of your teaching business. If you are a member of a teacher marketplace (see Chapter 2), billing and payment processing will typically be handled for you, and you will be able to withdraw your money, minus any service fees, to whatever online account you have designated (PayPal, Skrill, etc.). If you acquire students elsewhere, eg. via your website, you will need a more hands-on approach. It is good practice to charge students in advance of the lessons (see Chapter 5) as this ensures that you are paid for your services. In this chapter, we will cover payment processing and different methods of billing students.

Legal matters

If you are going to receive regular money transfers for services rendered, even via a teacher marketplace, you are legally required to set up a private company or register as a sole trader. Find a local accountant and ask about income tax, social security and VAT. If you are registered as self-employed, you can open a business bank account, which should facilitate tax and social security payments.

Online payment options

There are a number of online payment processors that integrate with your bank account and allow you to accept money online for your services safely and without your needing to write any code. The most popular service is PayPal, but there are several alternative methods that you might also want to consider.

Please note that these services often update their pricing, policies and interfaces, and the specific details or screenshots included in the following descriptions may become outdated at any time. Always check the website of the company for the most up-to-date information.

PayPal (PayPal.com)

Over 150 million people have an active PayPal account, allowing them to receive money instantly from other PayPal account holders in most countries of the world. To receive money from a PayPal user, the sender only needs an active PayPal account and your PayPal email address. You can withdraw your PayPal balance to your bank account at any time at no cost. If you receive money for goods or services, PayPal charges a transaction fee. At the time of writing, this is currently around 3.4% plus 20p per transaction for UK account holders with additional cross-border fees ranging from 0.4% to 1.5%. There is also an additional currency conversion fee of 2.5% above the wholesale exchange rate for converting your balance or payments that you receive into sterling. You can check the current fees for your country of residence by logging into your PayPal account and clicking 'Fees'.

Case study

Let's say you are based in the UK and you want to charge a Chinese student $200 USD for a package of lessons. Let's assume that the current wholesale currency conversion rate is 1.57 USD = 1 GBP, giving a GBP value of £127.73. The net amount that you would receive after PayPal's fees and currency conversion rates is calculated as follows:

Lesson package price / USD	$200 (£127)
PayPal percentage-based fee / USD	$6.80
Additional cross-border percentage-based fee / USD	$3
Fixed fee / USD	$0.30
Net amount / USD	$189.90
Net amount / GBP	£120.96
Net amount after PayPal conversion / GBP	£119.06

PayPal business account

If you are selling services online, you should sign up for a PayPal Premier or Business account. A business account is free and gives you valuable tools for requesting payment such as invoicing features and the ability to generate 'Buy now' buttons for your website. In addition, students will also be able to pay for your service by credit/debit card. Credit or debit card payments are still processed by PayPal but the payer does not need to be a PayPal account holder.

To sign up for a business account, go to www.paypal.com/signup/account.

Requesting money with PayPal

The easiest way to bill your students for lessons is to send a payment request. You can request a payment from anyone with an email address, even if they do not have a PayPal account. They will be able to pay with a credit/debit card if they don't want to sign up for a PayPal account. To send a payment request, click **Request Money** in the **Tools** box. Enter the recipient's email address, the amount you want to charge, select **Services** and click **Continue**.

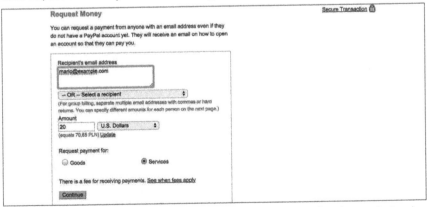

(Requesting payment with a PayPal business account, used with permission.)

Modify the email subject and include a message as needed. Click **Request Money** to send the email. The transaction will appear as a pending transaction in your PayPal balance until it is paid.

PayPal invoicing

Another way to bill students is to issue a PayPal invoice. Companies and self-employed individuals may request an invoice in order to claim your tuition service as a business expense. In order to generate an invoice, click **Invoicing** from the **Tools** box in your PayPal business account. You will be able to create an invoice template that you can reuse. You can add required information such as:

- the invoice number

- the due date

- your company name, address and logo (optional)

- the client's name, address and tax number if applicable

- the name of your service (eg. 'online English lesson' or 'online English tuition – 10 lesson credits')

- the quantity (number of lessons or packages)

- the unit price of each lesson or package

- any applicable tax/VAT.

It is your responsibility to create an invoice that is compliant with local laws and regulations, including the addition of the correct VAT rate, if applicable. Ask your accountant what information should be included in your invoices.

Generating PayPal links and buttons

If you have a website, you can include PayPal payment buttons that allow users to pay for your lessons. This looks more professional but requires adding some code to your webpage. Fortunately, PayPal offers a user-friendly interface for generating the payment button code.

In the header menu of your PayPal business account, select **Tools > Website Payments Standard** and click **Create a Button**. Select the button type **Buy Now** and enter the details of the service that you want to sell, including the name of the item (eg. '10 lesson credits'), an optional unique ID, the price and currency.

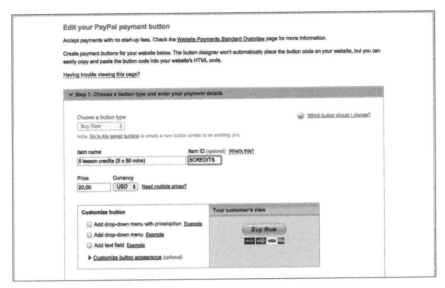

(Editing your PayPal payment button, used with permission.)

PayPal also allows you to automatically take clients to a special page when they have finished their checkout, for example a thank-you page displaying instructions on how to schedule their first lesson (see Chapter 3). To customise your checkout pages, click the banner 'Step 3: Customize advanced features (optional)'.

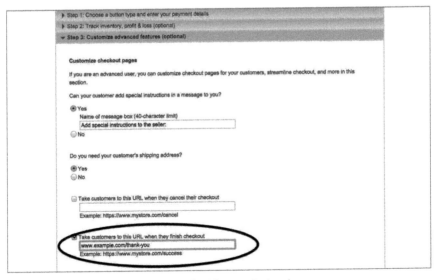

(Customising checkout pages, used with permission.)

After you have completed all the relevant fields, click **Create Button**. PayPal will generate two codes for you:

1. The code for your PayPal button to copy and paste into your website.

2. A payment link which you can send to customers by email.

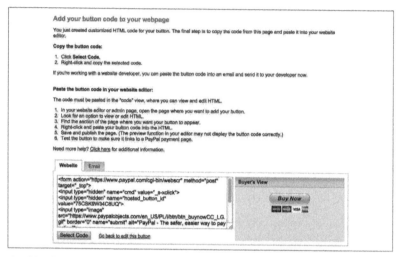

(Add a button code to your webpage, used with permission.)

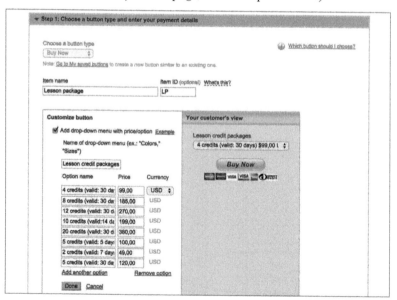

(Choose a button and add payment details, used with permission.)

You can also create a single payment button for all your different packages, allowing students to select the package they want from a drop-down menu. This can be achieved by checking the option 'Add drop-down menu with price/option' and entering the name and price of each item.

PayPal coverage

PayPal does not currently serve every country. As a result, residents of some countries will not be able to pay for your services. At the time of writing, these include Iran, Uzbekistan, Pakistan, Lebanon and Serbia. If any of these countries are important to you, you might consider offering a different payment method (see below). However, the availability of PayPal in countries does sometimes change.

2Checkout (2Checkout.com)

2Checkout operates in nearly every country in the world and makes it easy to accept payments from any device. The platform integrates with banks and payment networks all over the world through a single interface so you can sell to anyone, anywhere, in the local language and currency. You can quickly generate payment buttons for your website and accept payments by credit card, debit card or PayPal.

With 2Checkout, there is no need to prepare invoice templates manually, as buyers can click on a link provided in their payment confirmation emails if they need a bill for your service.

When it comes to withdrawing money, 2Checkout works a little differently from PayPal. With 2Checkout, your account balance is held until you reach a particular threshold, after which the money is sent to your bank account. To view 2Checkout's updated transaction fees, currency conversion rates and general policies, check their website.

In order to qualify for a 2Checkout account, you will need to submit an application, which will be reviewed by the company's underwriting team. To sign up, visit: www.2checkout.com/signup

Western Union (www.westernunion.com)

Western Union is a financial services company that allows you to transfer money to a bank account or for cash pickup in over 200 countries and territories. In order to send cash, the sender needs to:

- visit a local Western Union agent
- provide a valid form of identification
- complete a form with the receiver's name and city
- give the agent the cash plus a transaction fee
- collect a receipt with a Money Transfer Control Number, which may be required by the receiver.

The receiver then visits a local agent to collect the money. While not the most convenient way to pay for online services, Western Union can be useful in certain circumstances. For example, it may be useful if your student does not have a Visa or MasterCard, or if their country is not supported by your online payment processor.

Bank transfer

Most people use online banking, and requesting payment by bank transfer can be a convenient option if you are teaching students in your country of residence. Domestic bank transfers usually take around one-to-three business days in most countries. You can of course use PayPal for domestic payments. However, bear in mind that with a domestic bank transfer, you receive 100% of the lesson fee in your account. Requesting money by international bank transfer, on the other hand, is not recommended, as cross-border bank transfers are slow, expensive and inconvenient.

Billing

If you request payment by bank transfer, you may be required to send bills to your clients. Unless your business bank account provides an invoicing feature, you will need to use a third party billing tool. Fortunately, there are plenty of inexpensive online tools that enable you to quickly and easily create and send electronic bills, as well as generate monthly reports for accounting purposes. These tools will let you create and save an invoice template with your company address, bank account and logo so that you won't have to write out bills manually every time you request a payment. Ask your accountant about billing requirements.

At the end of this chapter there are a few suggested online accounting tools; however, you will probably be able to find a local invoice generator that is specially tailored to the billing requirements of your country of residence. Ask your accountant to recommend one.

Income declaration

Before the end of each month or taxation period, you will need to present your bills and invoices for expenses to your accountant for income declaration purposes. If you are processing payments on your website or via payment links, your accountant may only require proof of payment. Within a PayPal business account or a 2Checkout account, there are several reporting tools that allow you to generate lists of sales transactions as well as monthly income summaries. The lists will present the payment processor's fees and the net taxable amount, which you will need to declare.

Further reading and resources

PayPal alternatives

Five PayPal alternatives for small online businesses:
http://www.fairgroundmedia.com/paypal-alternatives

Free invoicing tools

Hiveage: http://www.hiveage.com/

Invoiced Lite: https://invoice-generator.com

Chapter 7:

Ideas and resources

Getting to know your students' needs, objectives, interests and levels intricately (see Chapter 5) will allow you to provide an optimum online learning experience. Many activities and lesson plans that work well in traditional one-to-one lessons will need to be adapted to the online environment. This chapter considers several ways of doing this, and looks at some additional resources suitable for online learning.

Teaching speaking

Many students look for an online tutor primarily to improve their speaking, and these students may prefer to learn exclusively through conversation. Generally, there should be little problem stimulating engaging discussions on a variety of issues. With some students, however, encouraging conversation in an authentic way may be a struggle. Below are some ideas for regular speaking activities, which you can use depending on the learning preferences of your student.

- Suggest a conversation topic for the next lesson and have the student prepare a talk.

- Allow the student to choose a topic that he or she finds interesting and stimulate a discussion.

- Ask the student to talk about a recent news event they have been following, an article they have read or documentary they have watched.

- Talk about an article that you have asked the student to read before the lesson.

- Talk about a video that you have asked the student to watch before the lesson.

- Talk about an article you have read, a place you have recently visited or a news report you have watched. Ask the student questions to stimulate a discussion.

- Share a picture and ask the student to describe the scene and the action. Follow up with a discussion related to the theme of the photo.

- Create online 'something to talk about' cards using a flashcard generator such as www.studystack.com. Use some default text for the blank side of the card ('Topic 1', 'Topic 2', 'Topic 3', etc.) and select topic titles for the reverse side ('My family', 'My last holiday', 'My ideal home', etc.)

You can consider mentioning the different options at the beginning of the course and allow the learner to indicate a preference. You will need to observe the student's level of enthusiasm carefully and experiment with different approaches when possible in order to keep the discussions engaging.

Correcting

You should employ helpful correction techniques that enable the student to learn from the conversations. A technique that most one-to-one teachers are familiar with is reformulation, that is, paraphrasing what the student says, after it has been said, in correct and natural English that is slightly above the student's level:

Student: I can to play the piano.

Teacher: You can play the piano? Nice.

This technique lends itself well to online learning and can also be used to improve the student's lexical resource:

Student: London is a very, very big city.

Teacher: Yes, I know. London is a huge city.

The advantage of using reformulation over spot or haphazard correction is that the flow of the discussion is uninterrupted and the conversation remains authentic. Google Sheets (see Chapter 1) can be used to keep a record of corrections. The spreadsheet will also serve as a something tangible to take away from the session and the notes can be used as the basis for a conversation and language recap.

You could experiment with various paraphrasing techniques. For example, if the student likes talking for long periods or if you are practising a long-turn speaking activity for an exam, it may be better to listen silently, take notes and paraphrase after the student has finished talking

Conversation recap

Asking the student to summarise the conversation using notes in a Google Sheet or Skype chat history is a great way to begin a new lesson. Apart from reinforcing the new language items introduced during the previous lesson, this ritual will give the student a real sense of progress and ultimately lead to a satisfied and loyal client.

Teaching writing

Many students may need to practise and improve their written English. Although writing tasks are often set for homework in order to focus on speaking during the lesson, you can experiment with collaborative writing activities. Using Google Docs (see Chapter 1) makes it possible to review the student's work online and provide feedback in a convenient way by adding comments.

Here are some ideas for writing tasks:

- Have a written conversation with the student in a Google Doc.
- Share a photo, for example an imaginary holiday postcard, and ask the student to write about it.
- Ask the student to write something spontaneously, for example, 'Write one thing you like about your work and one thing you dislike about it.'
- Ask the student to share an email he or she has written in English. Provide feedback and discuss language points.
- Assign a practical writing task, for example a job application letter, a complaint email, a product presentation, etc.
- Assign a narrative writing task, for example 'What I did last weekend'.
- Have the student write a short biography about someone famous.
- Have the student keep a journal in English.

Correcting

Google Docs comments can be used to highlight errors in a piece of writing. It is not necessary to correct every single mistake if there are a lot of errors; less confident students will find it disheartening to see most of their work highlighted in yellow. If you anticipate problems, you can agree in advance on the criteria for correction, for example, focus on spelling, vocabulary or an aspect of grammar.

One method of correction is to identify different types of mistakes and go through them with the student in the lesson. A coding system can be adopted if you don't want to type out the full words. Criteria could be abbreviated in the following way:

Grammar: *gr*

Word order: *wo*

Inappropriate vocabulary: *voc*

Wrong tense: *t*

Spelling: *sp*

Punctuation: *punct*

Alternatively, you can adopt a colour coding system, using the Google Doc text highlight feature.

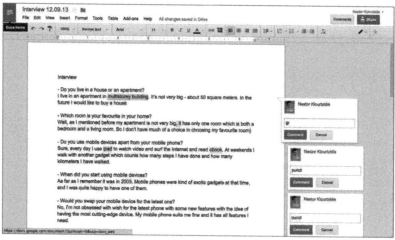

Highlighting errors in a Google Doc. (Google and the Google logo are registered trademarks of Google Inc., used with permission.)

If you choose not to discuss corrections during the lesson, comments in the Google Doc can be more detailed and used to jog the student's memory, for example: *Is this a countable noun or an uncountable noun?*

Using worksheets in online lessons

Online EFL lesson plans and worksheets can be used regularly with students who need or want a more conventional course incorporating reading, vocabulary exercises, grammar work, listening, speaking, pronunciation practice, etc.

There are literally hundreds of websites offering resources of varying quality. Some provide lesson plans that are 100% free to access and download, while others offer materials accessible only on payment of a subscription. While it is possible to provide a comprehensive course based exclusively on free resources, you should consider the following drawbacks:

- it can be more difficult to find what you are looking for

- the quality of free materials may be inferior

- free resources are usually less well-organised.

If you are still unsure whether it is worth paying for lesson plans, consider the extra time it would take you to source the same kind of materials for free. Multiply the estimated number of hours over the course of a year by the price of a lesson and compare to the cost of an annual subscription fee. Factor in the potential lost revenue as a result of devoting less of your time to marketing and the economic benefits become clear. However, before making any purchase, do make sure that the subscription licence covers sharing files with online students. Read the terms and conditions and contact the website if anything is unclear.

What kind of worksheets to look for

Downloadable worksheets are primarily designed for use in a classroom. In an online teaching context, they will work best if the student is able to print them out during or before the lesson. However, be aware that people are increasingly shunning home printing due to the convenience of digital transfers and mobile devices. You will therefore need to select materials that lend themselves to both digital and print formats.

Materials that tend to work better on screen will contain more imagery and less text than conventional worksheets. Supplementary multimedia resources such as videos and dialogues will additionally help stimulate the student. It is also convenient if the worksheets come with a student version and a teacher version. A student version of the worksheet (without teacher notes and answers) allows you to send the whole file without the need to use a pdf splitting tool to separate the sheets and remove the answer page.

Here are a few examples of websites that allow teachers to share downloadable lesson plans with online students. Visit each website to view their current prices for full membership.

Onestopenglish (www.onestopenglish.com)

Onestopenglish is run by Macmillan, a major publisher of English language teaching materials. This highly professional website boasts over 9,000 resources, including lesson plans, worksheets, audio, podcasts and flashcards. The materials are organised into core subject areas such as skills, grammar and vocabulary, business and ESP, exams and young learners. The pdf worksheets tend to be a little text-heavy so they will work best when printed out.

Key features

News lessons
These worksheets cover recent news items from the UK's *Guardian* newspaper, and are adapted to three levels. Each pdf handout contains reading practice as well as vocabulary, speaking and sometimes grammar work.

Vocabulary lesson plans
This extensive series of theme-based lesson plans and ideas is available in both American and British English. Many of the worksheets are free to try.

Business English worksheets
The Business English section of the website includes lesson plans based on articles from *Business Spotlight*, a bimonthly magazine for teachers and learners of English for business. Other useful series include 'Business tasks', a comprehensive set of worksheets covering functional language in business aimed at intermediate level and above, and 'Business skills', a short series covering essential skills such as emailing, telephoning, meetings and presentations.

Linguahouse.com

Linguahouse is an innovative website for both EFL learners and teachers. The site features hundreds of lesson plans for general and business English, including worksheets based on articles from the UK's *Independent* newspaper. Linguahouse boasts a number of features that lend themselves well to online teaching.

Key features

Audio and video
Many worksheets feature accompanying audio dialogues and video which can be played online in a number of ways:

- downloading the file and sharing it with the student

- playing the file online over Skype using a Skype add-on (see Chapter 1)

- sharing an online audio or video play link

- having the student scan a QR code in the worksheet with a mobile device or smartphone.

Course plans

Linguahouse worksheets are organised in a structured way, which also enables them to be used systematically as a complete course. This will help you devise a syllabus for your students. Course plans are available for all levels from elementary to advanced, and cater to general as well as business English needs.

Expemo

Expemo is an online flashcard application integrated with the Linguahouse website. The platform allows students to review the language from every worksheet in their own time. The tool minimises the time and effort needed for students to be able to permanently recall the learned material; it does this by using spaced repetition algorithms to personalise students' review schedules. As an online teacher, offering this kind of option to students may help you to stand out from the competition.

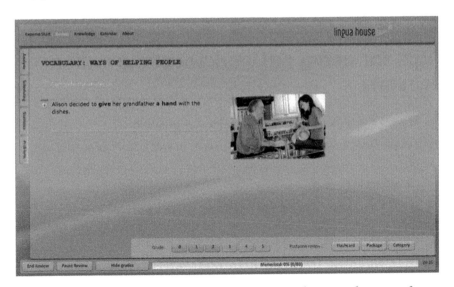

Example of an Expemo flashcard answer reviewing the target language from a worksheet.

Handoutsonline (www.handoutsonline.com)

Handoutsonline is an EFL resource site containing over 400 downloadable worksheets. Most use American English, although lesson plans generally feature a British English version as well. Worksheets currently cater to three levels: elementary, intermediate and advanced. As an online teacher, you would need to purchase an extended licence that allows you to share the resources in your online lessons and access student versions of the worksheets.

Handoutsonline worksheets have a simple format and clear design. The length of the lesson plans is a little on the short side, so to fill up a 50-minute lesson you will need to incorporate plenty of conversation or use more than one worksheet.

Key features

Business English

Handoutsonline includes a range of business English worksheets covering topics from practical business situations, desk work, people profiles, business issues, reading activities and grammar practice.

Theme lessons

These lesson plans can be used to stimulate discussions. The worksheets incorporate discussion, dialogues, role plays and vocabulary.

Tips for using pdf worksheets in online lessons

- Have the student print out the worksheet if possible.

- Utilise Google Sheets to make a record of answers and target language.

- Share your screen if you anticipate confusion over instructions (see Chapter 1).

- If the worksheet includes a key, consider using a pdf splitter (eg. www. splitpdf.com) to remove the answer pages before sharing the file with the student.

- If the worksheet contains an article or reading passage, consider extracting the text with a pdf splitter and sending the file to the student before the lesson.

Lesson plans designed for online teaching

EFL content providers have so far been slow to catch up with the rising demand for online teaching resources. This is likely to change as one-to-one online teaching continues to grow in popularity. Off2Class is one website that has attempted to meet the needs of online English teachers.

Off2Class (www.off2class.com)

Off2Class provides lesson plans for online private tutors covering grammar, vocabulary, spelling and speaking. Activities are presented as online slides which the teacher shares with students, allowing them to follow each lesson in real time from their own devices. This eliminates the need for VoIP screen sharing, transferring files and unnecessary instructions. Each lesson plan comes with instructions and answers that are hidden from the student, and the teacher is in full control of the learner's slides.

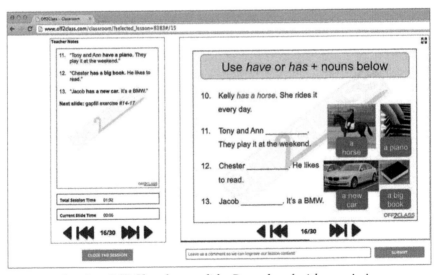

An example of an Off2Class lesson slide. Reproduced with permission.

Other EFL resources

A number of other websites provide resources for special activities and discussions. Below are two free websites that you might find useful.

Film English (www.film-english.com)

Film English is an award-winning website with over 120 ready-made lesson plans based on short films and videos. Each lesson includes plenty of speaking activities and additional exercises to do before and after watching each video. All the resources are free to use, but the site does ask for donations. Films are embedded in the website but they can be shared via links.

Breaking News English (www.breakingnewsenglish.com)

Despite its outdated and cluttered design, Breaking News English is considered by many teachers to be a good resource for incorporating authentic news into a one-to-one course. Lesson plans are based on an adapted current news story and include an extensive range of accompanying exercises. However, the biggest strength of this website is the adapted news items that are published every two days and graded at seven levels. These can be given to students as a basis for your own discussions and activities if you don't want to use the accompanying exercises.

Exam preparation resources

Throughout the year, millions of English students around the world are required to achieve a sufficient score in an accredited exam for immigration, study or career purposes. Due to the importance of these exams, many students will seek professional online tuition, particularly for the speaking section. Speaking test preparation is well suited to online learning with the teacher playing the role of the examiner and using reformulation to provide corrections and improve the student's lexical resource.

If you are intending to offer exam preparation tuition, you should familiarise yourself with the format and marking conventions of these tests. The following tests are the most popular accredited tests together with useful links and resources that you can use in your lessons.

IELTS

IELTS (International English Language Testing System) is an increasingly popular test of English language proficiency required for immigration and entry to universities in the UK and other countries. There is no pass or fail in IELTS. Candidates are graded on their performance using scores (bands) from 1 to 9 for each part of the exam. Since IELTS is a standardised international test, both British English and American English are recognised.

Finding a test centre: https://www.ielts.org/book-a-test/how-do-i-register

Prepare for IELTS: https://takeielts.britishcouncil.org/take-ielts/prepare

Sample tests and resources:

IELTS buddy: www.ieltsbuddy.com

IELTS-exam.net: www.ielts-exam.net

IELTS Blog: www.ielts-blog.com

Good Luck IELTS: www.goodluckielts.com

IELTS Speaking Test Generator: www.ieltsgenerator.com

British English exams

Cambridge English: B2 First
Cambridge English: B2 First, formerly known as Cambridge English: First (FCE), is an upper-intermediate level qualification. It proves that the learner can use everyday written and spoken English for work or study purposes.

Exam dates: www.cambridgeenglish.org/exams/first/exam-dates

Format: www.cambridgeenglish.org/exams/first/whats-in-the-exam

Cambridge English: C1 Advanced

C1 Advanced, formerly known as Cambridge English: Advanced (CAE), is an in-depth assessment of English for people who want to use English in demanding work and study situations.

Exam dates: www.cambridgeenglish.org/exams-and-qualifications/advanced/exam-dates/

Format: www.cambridgeenglish.org/exams-and-qualifications/advanced/whats-in-the-exam/

Cambridge English: C2 Proficiency

Cambridge English: C2 Proficiency, formerly known as Cambridge English: Proficiency (CPE), is Cambridge's most advanced qualification. It proves that the learner has achieved an exceptional level in English.

Exam dates: www.cambridgeenglish.org/exams-and-tests/proficiency/exam-dates/

Format: www.cambridgeenglish.org/exams-and-qualifications/proficiency/whats-in-the-exam/

American English exams

TOEFL

TOEFL (Test of English as a Foreign Language) is a widely recognised test designed to measure the ability of non-native speakers of English to use and understand North American English as it is spoken, written and heard in college and university settings. There are two formats: TOEFL PBT, administered in a paper-based format, and TOEFL iBT, administered via the internet. The former is being phased out.

Exam dates: www.ets.org/bin/getprogram.cgi?test=toefl

Speaking test format: www.goodlucktoefl.com/1-2-3-TOEFL_speaking.html

Resources and sample papers

Good Luck TOEFL: www.goodlucktoefl.com

ETS TOEFL: www.ets.org/toefl

TOEIC

TOEIC (Test of English for International Communication) measures the ability of non-native English-speaking candidates to use English in everyday workplace activities. TOEIC is used to hire and promote employees.

Resources and sample papers

ETS TOEIC: www.ets.org/toeic

Exam comparison

This useful table gives an approximate comparison between the different exams:

www.examenglish.com/examscomparison.php

Other useful resources

This website provides general information, resources and sample papers for most of the accredited English language tests:

Exam English: www.examenglish.com

Conclusion

Online tutoring is still in its development stage, but a regular search on Google will help you find many more suggestions shared by successful teachers. Keeping abreast of the latest methodology and experimenting with different approaches will help you grow in confidence as an online teacher. This confidence will shine through your marketing, consultations and trial lessons, enabling you to convert more prospective students into paying clients and consequently become a successful online English teacher.

Appendix

Running more than one Skype account simultaneously

If you are using a desktop or laptop, you can run more than one Skype account on the same computer at the same time by following these steps:

For Windows

1. From the Windows taskbar, click **Start > Run** (or press the Windows key and **R** keys on your keyboard at the same time).

2. In the **Run** window, type the following command (including the quotes) and press **OK**:

For 32-bit operating systems:
"C:\Program Files\Skype\Phone\Skype.exe" /secondary

For 64-bit operating systems:
"C:\Program Files (x86)\Skype\Phone\Skype.exe" /secondary

If you get an error message, copy and paste the exact command from this page and try again.

Be aware that if you've changed the installation path for Skype, then you'll need to enter the correct path for the **Skype.exe** file.

If the above solution fails, you can try another option:

1. Find the **Skype.exe** file in **C:\Program Files\Skype\Phone** if you're running a 32-bit operating system.

   If you're running 64-bit operating system, you can find the file in **C:\ Program Files (x86)\Skype\Phone**.

2. Right-click the file and select **Send to > Desktop** (create shortcut).

3. Locate the shortcut on your desktop, then right-click it and select **Properties**.

4. In the Target field of the Shortcut tab, add /secondary to the end of the path. The Target field should now be **"C:\Program Files\Skype\Phone\ Skype.exe" /secondary**.

5. Click **OK**. You can now start a new instance of Skype every time you double-click the new shortcut.

(Source: https://support.skype.com/en/faq/fa829/how-can-i-run-two-skype-accounts-on-the-same-computer)

For Mac

1. Open a Terminal window

2. Type sudo /Applications/Skype.app/Contents/MacOS/Skype and press Enter.

3. Enter your admin password when asked.

(Source: http://community.skype.com/t5/Mac/Run-two-skype-accounts-on-Mac-OSX-10-6-8/td-p/268772)